JACKSON
The Good Life

JACKSON
The Good Life

By Walt Grayson and Gil Ford Photography, Inc.

Profiles in Excellence and Captions by
Marlo Carter Kirkpatrick

Art Direction by
Robert Shatzer

URBAN
TAPESTRY
SERIES
TOWERY
PUBLISHING, INC.

LIBRARY OF CONGRESS CATALOGING-IN-PUBLICATION DATA

Grayson, Walt, 1949-
    Jackson : the good life / by Walt Grayson and Gil Ford Photography
Inc. ; profiles in excellence and captions by Marlo Carter
Kirkpatrick ; art direction by Robert Shatzer.
        p.   cm. — (Urban tapestry series)
    Includes index.
    ISBN 1-881096-57-2 (alk. paper)
    1. Jackson (Miss.)—Civilization. 2. Jackson (Miss.)—Pictorial
works. 3. Business enterprises—Mississippi—Jackson.
I. Kirkpatrick, Marlo Carter. II. Gil Ford Photography Inc.
III. Title. IV. Series.
F349.J13G725   1998
976.2'51—DC21   98-22098

Towery Publishing, Inc., 1835 Union Avenue, Memphis, TN 38104

PUBLISHER: J. Robert Towery
EXECUTIVE PUBLISHER: Jenny McDowell
NATIONAL SALES MANAGER: Stephen Hung
MARKETING DIRECTOR: Carol Culpepper
PROJECT DIRECTORS: Robert Philips, Beth Yerger
EXECUTIVE EDITOR: David B. Dawson
MANAGING EDITOR: Michael C. James
SENIOR EDITORS: Lynn Conlee, Carlisle Hacker
EDITORS/PROJECT MANAGERS: Mary Jane Adams, Lori Bond
EDITORS: Jana Files, Susan Hesson, Brian Johnston

ASSISTANT EDITOR: Rebecca Green
EDITORIAL ASSISTANTS: Allison Ring, Sunni Thompson
CREATIVE DIRECTOR: Brian Groppe
PROFILE DESIGNERS: Laurie Beck, Kelley Pratt, Ann Ward
DIGITAL COLOR SUPERVISOR: Brenda Pattat
DIGITAL COLOR TECHNICIANS: Jack Griffith, Darin Ipema, Jason Moak
PRODUCTION RESOURCES MANAGER: Dave Dunlap Jr.
PRODUCTION ASSISTANTS: Geoffrey Ellis, Enrique Espinosa, Robin McGehee
PRINT COORDINATOR: Tonda Thomas

CONTENTS

By Walt Grayson

CROSSROADS ARE AWFULLY POWERFUL PLACES IN southern lore and superstition. Almost every fire-breathing evangelist, at some time or another, has preached his share of sinners to the curbs of the crossroads of eternity. One avenue is the broad way that leads to destruction, and the other, the straight and narrow that leads to life. Hopefully, the poor lost soul looks both ways and chooses the correct direction.

Then again, there is no telling how many other pilgrims, instead of finding God, have sold their souls to the devil at a crossroads, either figurative or literal, for some gain they thought they couldn't attain on their own. Mississippi Blues legend Robert Johnson is supposed to have made just such a dark deal (where U.S. 61 crosses Highway 49) in exchange for fame and fortune. So it *can* be done.

I am pretty sure whoever came up with Jackson's "Crossroads of the South" slogan had neither of these scenarios in mind. It seems apparent that the Jackson/Crossroads connection came about because Highways 80 and 51 intersect here, making some reference to the most obvious identity for a place that, otherwise, is pretty difficult to get a handle on.

By the way, if the original routes for the interstate system had been adhered to, Jackson would have lost the essence of even *that* claim to fame in our day of the superhighway. Then-Mayor Allen Thompson managed to persuade Washington to let Interstate 55 intersect with Interstate 20 in Jackson, rather than have I-55 follow more closely the route of Highway 61 to the west, as was originally intended. "Just a holler from the crossroads of the South" doesn't sing quite like the more familiar slogan we grew up with.

The near crisis over the placement of the interstate is typical of the trials Jackson has had to tolerate while trying to extract some respect for itself from a very critical world. Mean-spirited folks used to say, "There ain't but three real towns in Mississippi: Memphis, New Orleans, and Mobile." The barb—aimed at Jackson

IT'S LITTLE WONDER THAT JACKSON IS OFTEN CALLED THE CROSSROADS OF THE SOUTH. TWO INTERSTATES, FIVE HIGHWAYS, AND A HISTORIC NATIONAL PARKWAY ALL CONVERGE IN THE CAPITAL CITY, LEADING TO A MULTITUDE OF ADVENTURES IN EVERY DIRECTION.

JACKSON WAS ORIGINALLY KNOWN AS LeFleur's Bluff, named in honor of Louis LeFleur, a Frenchman who operated a trading post on the bluffs above the Pearl River in the early 1800s. Because of the site's fertile soil, ample timber, and easy access to water transportation, LeFleur's Bluff was chosen for Mississippi's capital in 1821.

in particular and Mississippi in general—may have stung because there was an element of truth in it.

Delta folks have long considered Memphis their capital of sorts. And southwest Mississippians often head to the Crescent City to kick up their heels. I don't know for sure what they do in Mobile, but it gets its share of regular visitors from southeast Mississippi counties.

Any true Jacksonian bristles at such treason. But when pressed by the question, "Well, what *is* so great about Jackson?" we're stuck for superlatives. We don't have the South's tallest buildings or the largest population or the most money. Yet there are hundreds, maybe thousands, of things about this town that we like, or we wouldn't bother to live here, right?

But the truth of the matter is, it's tough to conjure up an encompassing personality for Jackson along the lines of, say, the persona of New Orleans. Our town has had this identity problem since it was founded.

And make no mistake: Jackson was, literally, found(ed). In 1820, the Choctaw Nation ceded a huge chunk of its lands in central Mississippi to the federal government. It was decided that, with all

that new territory opening up for settlement, the state capital ought to be in a more central location than way down south in Columbia, which was serving temporarily as the seat of government.

So, a search party headed by Thomas Hinds started up the Pearl River to find a suitable site. And when they got to the area where French trader Louis LeFleur had at one time operated a trading post (located about where South State intersects with Silas Brown), they liked what they saw. With bluffs rising above flood level on the west side of the river and fertile plains situated to the east, the area was perfect for settlement. This, they knew immediately, was the spot.

They surveyed the plan for the city, named it for Andrew Jackson (under whom Hinds had served in the War of 1812), and built a two-story brick statehouse, located near what is now the corner of Amite and President. All that was left to do was to step out of the way of all the people who would flock to the new capital to seek their fortunes and sink roots and grow lives.

And the people stayed away in droves. Baseball great Yogi Berra, addressing a different but similar situation a century and a half later, put this same spirit of indifference into words more eloquently than

THE "NEW" STATE CAPITOL WAS CON-
STRUCTED IN 1903 ON THE GROUNDS OF
THE OLD STATE PENITENTIARY. LEGENDS
PERSIST THAT THE PRISON WALLS WERE
TOO STRONG TO BE TORN DOWN IN SPOTS,
AND THAT PORTIONS OF THE ORIGINAL
STRUCTURE ARE STILL HIDDEN IN THE
LANDSCAPED GROUNDS SURROUNDING
THE OPULENT CAPITOL.

anyone before or since when he observed, "If people don't want to come out to the ballpark, nobody's going to stop them."

What "didn't stop" the prospective newcomers from coming to Jackson was simply that the towns and countryside along the Mississippi River had already attracted the lion's share of the available citizenry, and few of those who were comfortably settled saw a need to move inland to a fever-infested swamp, even if it was the capital city.

Besides, it wasn't a sure thing that Jackson would last as the capital for very long. In its first 25 or so years of existence, when the legislature wasn't in session, things were mighty quiet in Jackson. And when it *was* in session, one item that always came up was a measure to relocate state government to a bigger, more accessible, more wealthy, or more lively-after-dark kind of town.

This let's-move-the-capital fever became so bothersome that a moratorium was finally enacted prohibiting folks from bringing up the question until after 1850. By that time, people had pretty much gotten used to the place, and had forgotten about their itch to dump Jackson back into the Pearl. So, the city remains what it was created to be.

Dr. Eugene Farr, a Bible professor at Mississippi College in Clinton, used to tell his classes a little yarn about one of those attempts to oust Jackson. One of the by-products of that particular failed coup was a long-lasting feud between the normally friendly town of Clinton

and the nearby (and equally hospitable) village of Raymond.

The story goes that, in one of those early years of capitaldom, Clinton was to have been the benefactor of one of the pushes to get out of Jackson. Clinton is on the Natchez Trace and was the town through which most of the legislators had to travel to get to Jackson anyway. Plus, Clinton had fresh springwater and was already a sizable, thriving community. When they got around to voting on it, the initiative's final count revealed that it had fallen just one tally shy of enactment. The one ballot that killed the deal for Clinton had been cast by the representative from Raymond. So, a cold chill fell between the towns and lasted for decades.

Sure, that was a long time ago. However, Clinton has at least one souvenir of the episode—proof that Jackson didn't always have a lock on things. Farr always ended his story by pointing to a sign just outside his classroom window, there in Clinton, that read Capitol Street. The name hangs on to this day. Maybe they're still holding out hope.

But Clinton wasn't the only town left standing at the capital city altar. In doing the *Look Around Mississippi* series on WLBT over the years, I've run across about as many towns that (at least according to local legend) missed becoming the Emerald City by some small margin as I have houses that (at least according to their current owners) were pressed into use as field hospitals during the Civil War. And those stories—houses *and* towns—could all be true. ☞

MY FIRST PERSONAL EXPERIENCES WITH Jackson came in the 1950s, when my family would drive down from Greenville to see my aunt and uncle and cousins who lived here. Every so often, we'd go to the zoo or drive past Battlefield Park, where a real piece of the Civil War had taken place.

Four decades back, Jackson was a big deal for us out-of-towners. It's where Mama made an annual pilgrimage to the Baptist Book Store with her WMU circle. But Jackson also had shopping centers, while in Greenville we'd only heard of such things. Jackson even had a clover-leaf where State Street (then Highway 51) intersected Highway 80. Well, two leaves of a clover anyway. But two more than anywhere else in the state at the time.

In my childhood, Jackson was a great place to visit. Back then, there were woods behind my cousin's house on Maria Drive, complete with a crude playhouse/fort hidden deep within them. But in spite of forests in neighborhoods, I saw Jackson as the Big City, and the kids who lived there as having a big-city air about them. A touch of cockiness and conceit that comes from growing up in a place where it takes more than five minutes to drive from the farms on one side of town to the farms on the other side. An attitude of smugness that you get when you live in a town spread out enough that you could actually get lost in it. Later, as a teenager, I took my first solo overnight drive out of town to spend the night with my cousin in Jackson. We must have put a hundred miles on the car, just cruising back and forth between Shoney's at Westland Plaza and the Hulla-baloo in the Mart 51 shopping center. I always got turned around, and he had to tell me "left" or "right" at every intersection.

The next day, on my way back home, I felt a little more grown up. Not because we had actually done anything adult. But because I had been to the Big City by myself. ☞

ENRIQUE ESPINOSA

JACKSON IS CENTRALLY LOCATED WITHIN
500 MILES OF 2.5 MILLION BUSINESS AND
INDUSTRIAL CUSTOMERS—JUST A DAY'S
DRIVE FROM NEARLY HALF THE U.S.
MARKET.

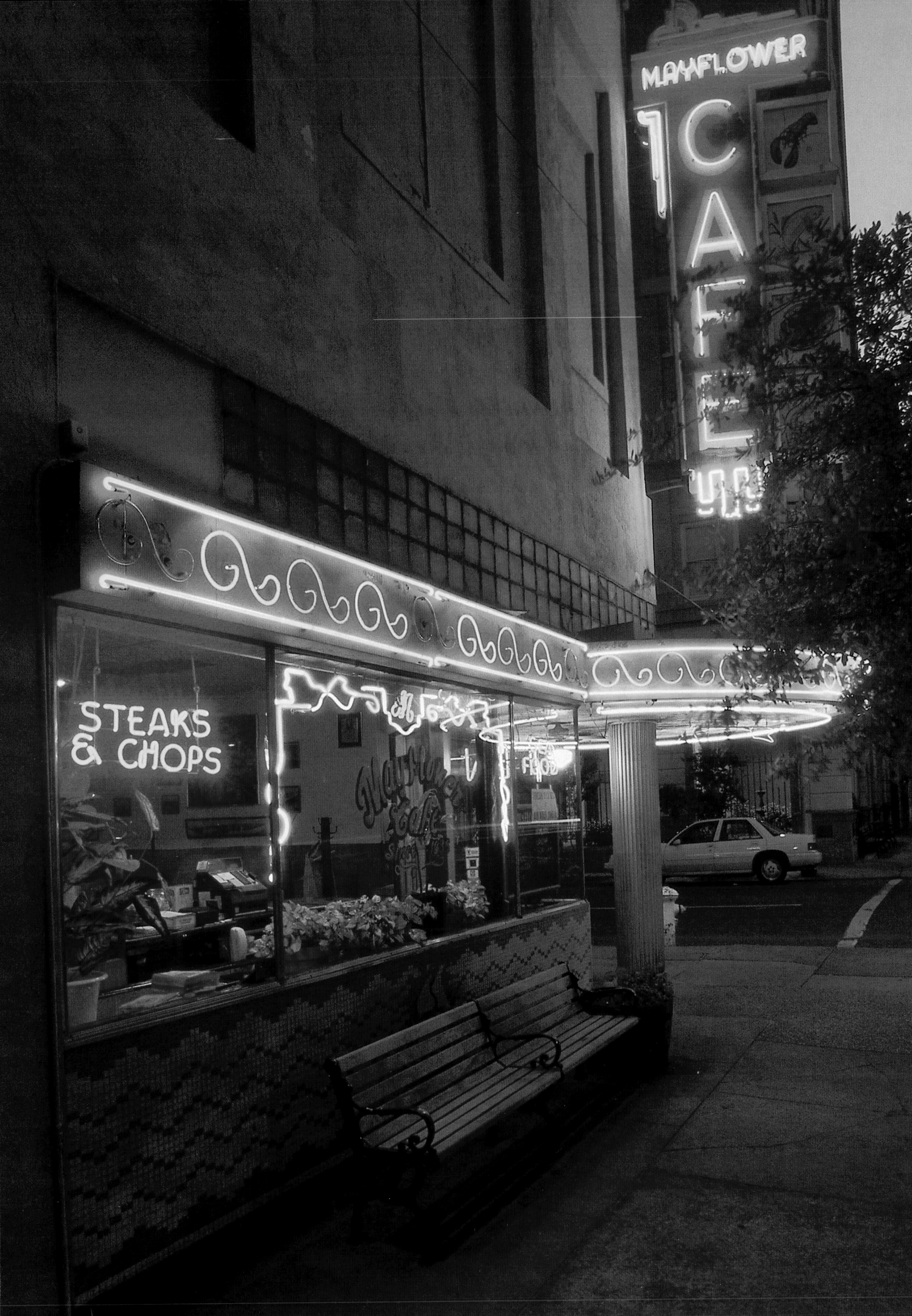

JIMMY WINSTEAD

AND FOR ME, JACKSON HAS ALWAYS BEEN THE BIG CITY. With the Standard Life and Lamar Life buildings and the towers of First National and Deposit Guaranty banks, there were plenty of skyscrapers in town. ✳ But even with the big-city trappings being built and paved here, for most other folks, Jackson's aura has always been a little more fuzzy. "It's just a big ole country town" was used more often than not to describe Jackson back then. And while it was bigger than any other town in the state, those of us who had lived in the country knew that Jackson wasn't a country town. I suppose whoever came up with that idea was trying to place Jackson where they thought it belonged—in the Grand Southern Myth of genteel mannerisms and blooming magnolias and mint juleps and always-charming folk with slow accents and good table manners.

Jackson grew out of its Southern Belle status rather quickly in the early 1960s. And it was the media revolution of the mid-20th century that helped it to do so. Ever since the first television sets came into our homes, most of us have relied on the box for the information that we use to form our opinions about almost everything in the world.

Because Greenville was in a fringe reception area, about all our TVs could get most of the time was snow and hiss. Out of necessity, then, came cable— not to bring us HBO or the Superstation, but to make our TV reception possible in the first place.

After the cable folks had strung the wire out North Broadway and into the back of our Magnavox, among the five choices on our dial were Jackson's two stations. Needless to say, we all started getting a clearer picture of the Big City. ☞

FOR A CONTEMPORARY SOUTHERN CITY, JACKSON BOASTS A DISTINCT RETRO FLAIR. THE ART DECO STANDARD LIFE BUILDING FIRST LIT UP THE SKYLINE IN 1929, WHILE THE NEON LIGHTS AND VINYL BOOTHS OF THE MAYFLOWER CAFE HAVE BECKONED TO DOWNTOWN DINERS SINCE 1935.

JIMMY WINSTEAD

TOM ROSTER

FRANK MELTON, PRESIDENT AND CEO OF
TV-3 INC., WHICH OWNS WLBT-TV,
TACKLES JACKSON'S TOUGHEST ISSUES IN
HIS HARD-HITTING, NO-HOLDS-BARRED
Bottom Line SEGMENTS. MELTON'S
AGGRESSIVE COMMENTARIES HAVE
EARNED HIM BOTH DEATH THREATS
AND NOMINATIONS FOR GOVERNOR.

It became a near-mystical experience for me to turn on the TV and, right there at my house in Greenville, see things happening in Jackson. The mechanics of the process weren't mystical. I understood waves and modulation. It was the medium itself that was magical. Every day at noon, Bob Neblett read us the *Jackson Daily News* on Channel 12, way before the paperboy tossed it into the driveway. (He even showed us a close-up of the Hennie cartoon at the bottom of the front page.)

And, of course, the dean of weathermen, Woodie Assaf, was right there on-screen. Woodie has been a fixture on WLBT from day

one; every time he steps in front of the camera to do another show, he sets a new world's record for the most weathercasts given by any one person.

While still a child in Greenville, I had no idea that I would ever become a part of the Jackson broadcasting community, much less spend the better part of 30 years here working at several radio stations, and now at WLBT. Nor did I have any notion that I would be fortunate enough to work with Woodie, and with other legends of the local airwaves, like WSLI's "Farmer" Jim Neal. ☛

DURING THE 1960S, CONFLICTS AT JACKSON'S SEGREGATED LUNCH COUNTERS WERE BROADCAST INTO HOMES AROUND THE COUNTRY. TODAY, THE CIVIL RIGHTS MOVEMENT AND ITS IMPACT ON MISSISSIPPI ARE CHRONICLED IN A PERMANENT EXHIBIT AT THE OLD CAPITOL MUSEUM.

ALTHOUGH I BELIEVE THAT MY RECOLLECTIONS of Jackson during my formative years are pretty accurate, everyone has different experiences. It has been said that the truth has many faces and many voices. Here's what three other folks recall about Jackson in years gone by. ✳ The first is Lerone Bennett, editor of *Ebony* magazine, who grew up in Jackson a few decades earlier than I came on the scene—of another race and in a different part of town. His house was a little bungalow on Pearl Extended, located just the other side of the Illinois Central tracks from downtown. Years later, as *Ebony's* editor, Bennett recalled what it was like for him growing up in Jackson. Fear was the backdrop of almost every activity in his community—fear of who would come along and do something to a people who had little voice about what was done to them.

IN AND AROUND JACKSON, THE FINE ART OF SOUTHERN LIVING THRIVES, TUCKED AWAY ON THE FRONT PORCHES AND BEHIND THE SCREENED DOORS OF THE CITY'S CLOSE-KNIT NEIGHBORHOODS.

Bennett tells of a Jackson where neighborhood watch was in practice long before it had a name, because survival itself depended on people watching out for one another. He said that this vigilance ranged from trying to prevent crime (of which there was relatively little) to correcting neighbors' children who were about to violate the unwritten code of things that just weren't done by good people.

The second source is Willie Morris, one of my all-time favorite Mississippi writers, who recalls Jackson around the same time as Bennett—the years of the Second World War. Back then, as a preteen, Morris made trips via Greyhound from Yazoo City to pay surprise visits to his grandpa Percy, who lived on Fortification Street in Jackson. Unlike Bennett, Morris had no problem going almost anywhere he wanted in those days, either unescorted or with his grandfather. Among his favorite excursions, he once told me, was the trip to buy black-market bubble gum on the lower end of Capitol in a little shop across the street from the

King Edward. Then, he'd pass the gum through the fence to a German POW at the Clinton military camp in exchange for a war-rationed commodity: a can of Pet Milk from the Red Cross. (Germans weren't the only foreigners here during World War II. Dutch airmen also trained here, and I understand they liked to buzz the houses of the pretty local girls.)

Then there's the grande dame of Mississippi writers, Eudora Welty, who has plenty of grand remembrances of her youth in Jackson. Confined to her bed during an extended childhood illness, she tells stories of hearing the laughter of children on the playground across the street at Davis School, or, on sultry summer evenings, of sleepily following the conversations drifting up to her open bedroom window from the neighbor's front porch swing just below. After Welty recovered, she used these and other memories to fashion her priceless stories of long-gone Jackson.

TOM ROSTER

Four childhoods: my Big City, Lerone Bennett's "village" that huddled together for safety, Willie Morris' place of high adventure, and Eudora Welty's bedroom, where she learned to observe the world. Four different impressions of the same place, separated only by time and perspective. And how many hundreds of thousands of people have lived here over the course of Jackson's history—each with his or her own particular viewpoint of the town, each different from any that I just mentioned?

The point is this: Contrary to popular perception, it's not as if our city has no personality. In fact, it has a plethora of them. When people think of Jackson, it's not in broad terms or grand visions, but in smaller images, one or two little things that happen to strike them at the moment. Even the great storyteller Charles Kuralt, who seemed able to sum up any place in a few choice words, was stumped when it came to Jackson; the best image he could come up with was that it was a city where you couldn't find anything to drink. (Had

WHILE EVERY JACKSON NEIGHBORHOOD HAS A DISTINCT PERSONALITY, ALL COME WITH AN EQUAL DOSE OF SOUTHERN CHARM (LEFT). PULITZER PRIZE-WINNING AUTHOR EUDORA WELTY, WHO WAS BORN IN THIS QUAINT VICTORIAN COTTAGE IN 1909 (OPPOSITE) AND WHO STILL MAKES HER HOME IN THE CAPITAL CITY, HAS INTRODUCED MANY READERS TO THAT ENCHANTING WAY OF LIFE THROUGH SUCH WORKS AS *Delta Wedding*, *The Optimist's Daughter*, AND *One Writer's Beginnings*.

someone simply taken him across the Pearl River to the Gold Coast, he would have found not only enough vodka to drown in, but also lots of material for one of his excellent reports.)

It's true: Jackson has had no one thing in particular that has galvanized the majority of its people (like a French Quarter or Graceland, for example). There's been little, if anything, to draw the city's essence from—no postcard image that says in one distinct blow that this is what we are, or who we are.

TOM ROSTER

To make it even more complicated, even the small things that people think of when they talk of Jackson are always changing. The Jackson that was my Big City is gone. Lerone Bennett's neighborhood doesn't exist anymore. Willie Morris' grandfather's house is now the parking lot for Jitney Jungle #14. And Eudora Welty's childhood home, where all those wonderful stories began to form themselves, is now an insurance office. Even the Gold Coast is no more. ☞

JACKSON IS OFTEN DESCRIBED AS A "BIG SMALL TOWN" OR A "GREAT PLACE TO RAISE A FAMILY," BUT THE TRUE ESSENCE OF THIS WARM AND WELCOMING COMMUNITY CAN BE BEST FOUND IN SNAPSHOTS OF DAILY LIFE.

SUCH CHANGE IS CERTAINLY RELENTLESS, AND it is anything but subtle. A friend of mine who grew up in Jackson, and who long ago transplanted himself to Orlando by way of a few years' stay in California, once remarked that in all of his return trips home over the years, he's never come back to the same city twice. Jackson to him is like a caterpillar, continually changing into a butterfly.

I am convinced that Jackson has not yet become what it will end up being recognized for. Someday, the city will be bestowed with the respect it has always sought. There are thousands and thousands of favorite things about Jackson to thousands and thousands of people.

What are some of those things? I remember a young announcer who worked with us back in the rock-and-roll days at WRBC. He was one of those wandering gypsies who drifted from town to town and station to station looking for perhaps more than another job, but not knowing what else it was he wanted—only knowing when he hadn't found it. And he didn't find it here.

He didn't particularly care for Jackson. He said there was no culture here. Poor boy. It was here back then, and it always has been. ☞

IN RECENT YEARS, JACKSON HAS SLOWLY BUT SURELY ESTABLISHED A REPUTATION AS A CENTER FOR THE ARTS. THE CITY HAS INSPIRED THE CREATIVE EFFORTS OF A NUMBER OF WELL-KNOWN TALENTS, INCLUDING PULITZER PRIZE-WINNING AUTHOR RICHARD FORD (OPPOSITE) AND RENOWNED POET, NOVELIST, AND LECTURER DR. MARGARET WALKER ALEXANDER (RIGHT).

H.K. HOLLOWAY

Why, this is where Eudora Welty penned her wonderful stories and from where she takes us to live at the P.O. with Sister, or to be swept off our feet by Natchez Trace robbers, or to a beauty shop to discuss the wonders of the Petrified Man.

From her writing room in Jackson, Margaret Walker Alexander explored her roots in *Jubilee*, inspiring Alex Haley to do the same.

Beth Henley put her Jackson experiences to paper, and brought them to life on Broadway and in the movies.

Ellen Douglas has fashioned a grand parade of outstanding novels about life in Jackson.

A little recording company out on Northside Drive has been quietly releasing to the world the music that was invented here in Mississippi. Since the mid-1960s, Malaco Records and its subsid-

iaries have covered the planet with down-home blues and its heavenly twin, gospel, as well as covering the charts with hits. Before them, back in the 1950s, was Ace Records, with rock and roll and its cousin, rhythm and blues.

Jackson is home of the Belhaven Singing Christmas Tree. The Toogaloo Choir. The Sonic Boom of the South (aka the Jackson State University Marching Band). The Mississippi Opera. The Mississippi Symphony.

And Jackson is the only city in the Western Hemisphere to host the USA International Ballet Competition, bringing top dancers from across the country and around the globe to vie for world honors.

Culture? It goes on and on. ☞

TURN ON THE RADIO, AND YOU'LL LIKELY HEAR A SONG THAT HAS ITS ROOTS IN MISSISSIPPI—THE BIRTHPLACE OF THE BLUES, COUNTRY MUSIC, AND THE KING OF ROCK AND ROLL HIMSELF, ELVIS PRESLEY. TODAY, THAT RICH MUSICAL HERITAGE IS CELEBRATED IN JACKSON EVERY DAY AND NIGHT.

WITH AN OFF-THE-CHARTS ENERGY
LEVEL, MOVES A CONTORTIONIST WOULD
ENVY, AND A BEAT THAT GETS YOU
DANCING IN YOUR SEAT, THE JACKSON
STATE UNIVERSITY MARCHING BAND—

THE SONIC BOOM OF THE SOUTH—
ATTRACTS AS MANY FANS AS THE
UNIVERSITY'S FOOTBALL TEAM. ALSO
GUARANTEED TO LIFT YOUR SPIRITS IS
THE BELHAVEN SINGING CHRISTMAS

TREE. TRIMMED IN TWINKLING LIGHTS,
THE HOLIDAY FAVORITE WARMS UP FROSTY
DECEMBER NIGHTS WITH TRADITIONAL
AND CONTEMPORARY CAROLS.

▶ HUBERT WORLEY JR.

BALLET HAS A STRONG FOLLOWING IN
JACKSON—HOME TO ITS OWN PROFES-
SIONAL COMPANY, BALLET MISSISSIPPI,
AND THE ONLY CITY TO HOST THE
PRESTIGIOUS USA INTERNATIONAL
BALLET COMPETITION.

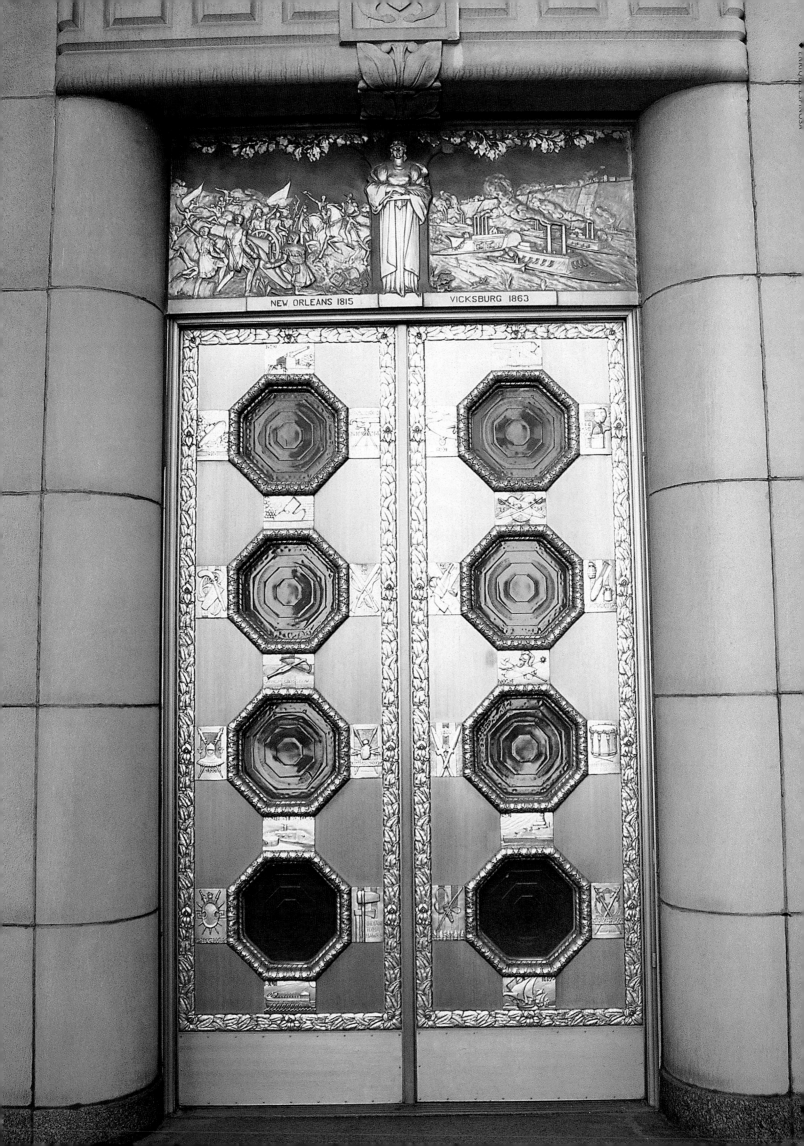

NEW ORLEANS 1815   VICKSBURG 1863

I HAD NOTICED, BUT NOT REALLY APPRECIATED, local architecture before my trip to St. Petersburg, Russia, to photograph that city's palaces in anticipation of Jackson's 1996 exhibition. So, park your car downtown sometime, get out and stroll around, and just look. ✳ Look at the War Memorial Building, especially the doors. And notice the reliefs flanking either side of the broad steps up to the tomb of our unknown soldier. The sculptor used the same model for all of the figures. Hence, they all look alike. Even the woman has the same face as the men.

Next door is the Old Capitol. At one time, it was in such deplorable condition that it was about to fall down. Renovation has saved the place, where notables from Jefferson Davis and Henry Clay all the way to Bill Clinton have stood in its halls or on its steps and taken a turn at swaying public opinion. There are even some pretty good ghost stories that center around the Old Capitol.

DEDICATED IN 1940, THE MISSISSIPPI WAR MEMORIAL BUILDING HONORS THE "MEMORY OF THOSE WHO FELL IN THE SERVICE OF THIS COUNTRY BY LAND AND BY SEA." HIGHLIGHTS INCLUDE A MILITARY MUSEUM, A SET OF CAST ALUMINUM DOORS DEPICTING SCENES FROM SEVERAL HISTORIC BATTLES, AND TWO INTRICATE MONUMENTS FEATURING LIFE-SIZE WAR FIGURES.

Jackson's columned City Hall is one of the few survivors of the Civil War that are still with us. Supposedly, General William Tecumseh Sherman, being a Mason, decided not to torch the building—not because it was an important civic center for the city, but because its third floor was a Masonic Hall. (By the way, once upon a time, the city wanted to evict the Masons so they could have more office space, but in searching the title to the building, they found that the Masons have a better claim to the structure than does the city itself.)

It's worth noting that Jackson is also where Sherman uttered his famous words, "War is hell." Most folks don't realize, though, that he didn't say this because of the carnage of the Vicksburg Campaign that was going on at the time, but instead because he lost a good team of mules and two cannons in the Pearl River just across the street from where WLBT is now located. ☛

DURING THE CIVIL WAR, UNION TROOPS
REDUCED JACKSON TO A SMOKING RUIN,
EARNING THE ONCE-LOVELY CITY THE
DISMAL NICKNAME CHIMNEYVILLE
(OPPOSITE). "WE HAVE MADE GOOD PROG-
RESS TODAY IN THE WORK OF DESTRUC-
TION," UNION GENERAL WILLIAM
TECUMSEH SHERMAN TOLD GENERAL
ULYSSES S. GRANT. "JACKSON WILL NO
LONGER BE A POINT OF DANGER." ONE
OF ONLY A HANDFUL OF BUILDINGS TO
SURVIVE THE CIVIL WAR TORCHING, CITY
HALL SERVED AS A HOSPITAL DURING THE
CONFLICT (ABOVE).

Another architectural highlight is the Governor's Mansion, one of the nation's oldest and most beautiful first residences. Across the street is the Lamar Life Building, guarded by its gargoyles and grotesques. At the other end of downtown is the art deco Standard Life building, a refugee from the Gilded Age.

The New Capitol was built on the foundations of the state's first prison (a touch of irony not lost on a number of pundits). What's more, the whole city was built atop an ancient volcano that was created, scientists now believe, by a meteor strike of all things.

There's much more, of course. There is a Frank Lloyd Wright house in Woodland Hills. There are the shadows of the first community built by freed blacks after the Civil War in the Farish Street Neighborhood Historic District. And, although it's not what you'd normally think of as architectural, a cypress swamp sits just to the south of the Pearl Street/Pascagoula Street entrances and exits to downtown. While there's talk of draining the area to make room for another strip of fast-food outlets, I, for one, hope it always stays a swamp. ☛

WHERE ELSE ON PLANET EARTH IS THERE the mix of races, religions, and superstitions like you'll find in the South? And with Jackson serving as the South's crossroads, for every plateful of "Southern" that you get elsewhere, a whole smorgasbord of it passes through here sooner or later.

The business of change in Jackson extends well beyond storytelling and music making. Jackson is an important crossroads in a social sense as well. It's no wonder that many of the gains that came from the civil rights movement of the 1960s were a result of ills brought to the attention of the world from Jackson lunch counters.

All of these elements and many more go into what comprises Jackson. Only when you put all of the parts together does a total picture emerge. While the parts may seem diminished when looked

▶ TOM ROSTER

UPON COMPLETION, THE MISSISSIPPI STATE CAPITOL WAS PROCLAIMED BY MANY TO BE THE "MOST PROMINENT PUBLIC BUILDING IN THE SOUTH." ITS 1903 DEDICATION WAS SO MONUMENTAL THAT THE NEW ORLEANS *Times-Democrat* PUBLISHED A 40-PAGE "MISSISSIPPI CAPITOL" EDITION, AND EVERY EXTRA PASSENGER CAR ON THE ILLINOIS CENTRAL RAILROAD SYSTEM WAS PUT INTO SERVICE TO ACCOMMODATE THE EXCITED CROWDS FLOCKING TO JACKSON.

at by themselves, when you go about trying to extract a definition of the city, it's like experiencing a kaleidoscope: It's the overall pattern formed from all of the many changing colors that you're really seeing.

And for Jackson, the pattern isn't yet fixed. The kaleidoscope is still turning, the individual colors are still mixing and relating to each other, and the new pattern that's called Jackson is constantly making itself over again and again with every passing day. ✳

Jackson's New State Capitol was designed by Theodore Link, a prominent architect from St. Louis who described the landmark as "a pure renaissance classic . . . which will fittingly express the power, honor, and stability of the state." The city's first all-electric building, the structure was a technological phenomenon, complete with ornate light fixtures to showcase the modern marvel of electricity. However, because some doubt existed as to whether this "newfangled invention" would really work, every third fixture was also equipped with a gas jet.

THE GOOD LIFE

WITH ELABORATE MOLDINGS AND PEDIMENTS (TOP), AND A MAJESTIC, SOLID COPPER EAGLE WITH A 15-FOOT WINGSPAN (OPPOSITE), THE BEAUX ARTS NEW CAPITOL REFLECTS THE HOPES AND ASPIRATIONS OF THE PAST, AS WELL AS THE PROGRESS AND VISION OF TODAY. ERECTED ON THE LAWN BY THE UNITED CONFEDERATE VETERANS, THE MONUMENT TO THE WOMEN OF THE CONFEDERACY PAYS TRIBUTE TO THOSE "WHOSE PIOUS MINISTRATIONS TO OUR WOUNDED SOLDIERS SOOTHED THE LAST HOURS OF THOSE WHO DIED FAR FROM THE OBJECTS OF THEIR TENDEREST LOVE" (BOTTOM).

City Hall was built by slave labor in 1846 for the then-exorbitant cost of $7,505. More than a century later, Katherine Rhymes Speed Ettl's statue of General Andrew Jackson was erected to commemorate the city's namesake. Today, "Old Hickory" greets visitors to City Hall from its location in the Josh Halbert Gardens, named in honor of Jackson's longtime city engineer.

DESIGNED BY WILLIAM NICHOLS, THE MISSISSIPPI GOVERNOR'S MANSION HAS BEEN HOME TO THE STATE'S CHIEF EXECUTIVE SINCE 1842, MAKING IT THE NATION'S SECOND-OLDEST CONTINUOUSLY OCCUPIED GUBERNATORIAL RESIDENCE (LEFT AND CENTER).

ENRIQUE ESPINOSA

On weekdays, downtown's Smith Park fills with professionals on lunch break, power walkers clad in business suits and sneakers, and other folks out to enjoy an afternoon in the sunshine.

Dedicated in 1930, the Hinds County Courthouse in Jackson has been described as a "temple of justice," a modern version of an ancient Greek temple. Standing watch over the building's entrances are sculptures of Moses, the giver of the law, and Socrates, the interpreter of the law.

JACKSON

There's a concentration of political power on High Street, home of the Carroll Gartin Justice Building, where the Mississippi Supreme Court holds sway, and the Walter Sillers Building, where a number of state agencies and offices keep the governmental workings of Mississippi on track.

GIL FORD PHOTOGRAPHY, INC.

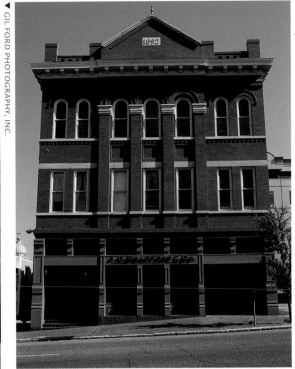

ENRIQUE ESPINOSA

GREGORY M. WILLIAMS

IN THE PAST FEW DECADES, MANY OF JACKSON'S HISTORIC STRUCTURES HAVE BEEN RESTORED OR RENOVATED FOR USE AS MODERN OFFICE SPACE, INCLUDING THE J.C. BRADFORD BUILDING (TOP RIGHT) AND THE HERITAGE BUILDING (TOP LEFT), BOTH ON CAPITOL STREET.

COMPLETED IN 1904, JACKSON'S CENTRAL Fire Station served as department headquarters until 1974, when a new station was erected. Three years later, the MetroJackson Chamber of Commerce renovated the old building as office space, and still makes its home in the historic structure (above and opposite bottom).

ARCHITECTURE IN DOWNTOWN JACKSON IS AN ECLECTIC MIX OF THE HISTORIC AND THE CONTEMPORARY. BUILT IN 1925 AND HAILED AS JACKSON'S FIRST "SKY-SCRAPER," THE 10-STORY LAMAR LIFE BUILDING AND ITS DISTINCTIVE CLOCK TOWER HAVE MAINTAINED AN UNMIS-TAKABLE PRESENCE IN THE CITY CORE; THOUGH DWARFED BY ITS HIGH-RISE NEIGHBORS, THE ORNATE TOWER, WITH ITS UBIQUITOUS AMERICAN FLAG, RE-MAINS A FOCAL POINT.

As Mississippi's capital city, Jackson is the center of commercial activity for the entire state. The business district surrounding One Jackson Place is home to accounting firms, advertising agencies, real estate groups, law firms, banks, and telecommunications companies (pages 56 and 57).

DISTINCTIVE ARCHITECTURE ABOUNDS IN AND AROUND JACKSON, FROM THE A.E. WOOD COLISEUM ON THE CAMPUS OF MISSISSIPPI COLLEGE IN CLINTON (ABOVE) TO THE UPSCALE LANDMARK CENTER, BUILT ON LAND ONCE DEEMED UNUSABLE DUE TO FLOODING (OPPOSITE).

It may not be what you'd call fine art, but some downtown signage has been around long enough to graduate from "tacky" to "vintage."

LOCATED IN THE HEART OF DOWNTOWN
ON EAST CAPITOL, THE ELITE RESTAU-
RANT HAS BEEN PLEASING THE PALATES OF
DISCERNING DINERS FOR MORE THAN 50

YEARS. OPENED IN 1947, THE COLORFUL
CAFÉ IS KNOWN FAR AND WIDE FOR ITS
SUMPTUOUS SOUTHERN FARE.

ENRIQUE ESPINOSA

ENRIQUE ESPINOSA

Downtown Jackson is home to several tried-and-true eateries whose owners have perfected the art of the blue plate special. Making a name for themselves around town are (clockwise from top left) Frank Latham of Frank's World Famous Biscuits, Mike Kountouris of the Mayflower Cafe, Peter Zouboukos of the Elite, and Allen Hart of Blue Cafe.

Each April, the International Red Beans and Rice Festival packs the lawn in front of One Jackson Place with live music and entertainment, costumed cooking teams, and more than your fill of (what else?) red beans and rice.

▲ ENRIQUE ESPINOSA

Widely considered Jackson's wackiest annual event, Mal's St. Paddy's Day Parade and Festival combines a traditional pub crawl with Mardi Gras-like festivities, including a trinket-tossing parade where the most outlandish float wins a prize, a street dance featuring several local bands, and plenty of other fun-filled activities. Past parade themes have included Sixteen Scandals, Irish I Was a Movie Star, and Elvis Was Irish.

68

You never know what you'll see during the St. Paddy's Day Parade, which features enough thrills and excitement to fire some up and make others green with envy.

JACKSON TAKES CARE OF ITS OWN—BIG OR
SMALL, YOUNG OR OLD, HUMAN OR FELINE.
HERE, A HEROIC FIREFIGHTER RESCUES
ONE OF THE CITY'S TINIEST RESIDENTS,
WHILE THE JACKSON ZOO HOSPITAL WEL-
COMES A HEALTHY CHEETAH CUB TO ITS
NEW HOME.

First opening its gates in 1919, the Jackson Zoo had been firmly established as one of the city's most popular attractions by the time these gators posed for the camera in the 1930s (left). Today, the zoo is home to an outstanding collection of wild animals and covers more than 100 sprawling acres of re-created natural habitats.

You don't have to venture outside the city limits to experience the area's spectacular wildlife. The swampy areas surrounding the Pearl River are home to countless reptiles and amphibians (opposite), and the wooded walking trails of LeFleur's Bluff State Park offer a tranquil, back-to-nature experience just steps from one of Jackson's busiest thoroughfares (left).

A short drive from Jackson, the town of Flora is home to the Mississippi Petrified Forest, which features giant tree trunks that are estimated to be between 36 and 50 million years old. The only such preserve in the eastern United States, it was designated a National Natural Landmark by the National Park Service in 1966.

The scenic Natchez Trace Parkway winds from Natchez to Nashville, following a path first trekked by Native Americans, pioneers, and the original Pony Express. Each October, the Mississippi Crafts Center in Ridgeland holds the Pioneer and Indian Festival, celebrating the history of the Trace with crafts, traditional food, and live history demonstrations.

Housed in an old dogtrot log cabin, the Mississippi Crafts Center displays and sells work by members of the Craftsmen's Guild of Mississippi, including basketry, woodworking, pottery, and jewelry. The crafts center also stages live demonstrations of such traditional activities as whittling, weaving, carving, and quilting.

NAMED FOR A FORMER STATE COMMIS-
SIONER OF AGRICULTURE, JACKSON'S JIM
BUCK ROSS MUSEUM COMPLEX, AFFEC-
TIONATELY CALLED THE AG MUSEUM,
INCLUDES LIVING HISTORY RE-CREATIONS
OF SMALL-TOWN LIFE IN THE 1920S.

For more than half a century, the Mississippi Symphony Orchestra has thrilled listeners of all ages with a mix of classical, chamber, and pops concerts. In addition to the master-pieces performed under Maestro Colman Pearce, conductor from 1987 through the 1998-1999 season (opposite, top left), audiences have enjoyed such renowned guests as entertainer Dudley Moore, pianist Alon Goldstein, and singer Toni Tennille (opposite, top right).

JACKSON'S LANDSCAPES, ARCHITECTURE, AND SOUTHERN PERSONALITY HAVE IN- SPIRED A NUMBER OF PROFESSIONAL AND AMATEUR ARTISTS. RENOWNED WATER- COLORIST WYATT WATERS (OPPOSITE) IM- MORTALIZED MANY OF THE CAPITAL CITY'S STREETSCAPES AND LANDMARKS IN HIS BOOK *Another Coat of Paint*.

Downtown Jackson's Farish Street and its environs were once the hub of African-American business, commerce, and entertainment. Today, efforts are under way to preserve and promote the Farish Street Neighborhood Historic District as a cultural center and tourist attraction.

Housed in the state's first school for African-American children, the Smith Robertson Museum and Cultural Center celebrates the contributions of African-Americans to education, politics, and the arts in Mississippi.

A downtown landmark for a century and a half, the Old Capitol was the center of state government for more than 60 years. In recognition of the building's historic signifi-cance, artist Victoria Monk was commissioned to paint this mural on a bridge near Mill Street as part of a downtown beautification project.

88

The Old Capitol Museum today houses exhibits chronicling state history from Mississippi's settlement by Native Americans through the civil rights movement. The real attraction, however, is the building itself—a magnificent Greek Revival statehouse designed by architect William Nichols and completed circa 1840.

LOCATED ADJACENT TO THE OLD CAPI-
TOL MUSEUM, THE MISSISSIPPI WAR
MEMORIAL BUILDING HONORS THE
STATE'S MEN AND WOMEN WHO HAVE
GIVEN THEIR LIVES FOR THEIR COUNTRY.
OUTSIDE THE STRUCTURE IS THE TOMB
OF THE UNKNOWN SOLDIER (RIGHT)
AND TWO SCULPTURE GROUPS DEPICTING
LOCAL CITIZENS AT WAR AND AT PEACE
(OPPOSITE BOTTOM).

Mississippi was the site of several pivotal battles during the Civil War. More than a century later, folks in and around Jackson remember that significant past through reenactments. In nearby Edwards, locals relive the 1863 Battle of Champion Hill—a Confederate loss that led to the fall of Vicksburg, which ultimately cost the South the war.

Only a handful of antebellum homes survived General Sherman's torching of Jackson during the Civil War. This historic mansion on State Street, complete with a vintage cannon out front, has been renovated for modern use as office space.

With its ornate headstones and solemn atmosphere, historic Greenwood Cemetery is the final resting place for many Jacksonians who died before the Civil War.

THE 1857 MANSHIP HOUSE WAS THE HOME OF CHARLES HENRY MANSHIP, JACKSON'S CIVIL WAR-ERA MAYOR. AN EARLY PRACTITIONER OF ORNAMENTAL PAINTING, MANSHIP SPECIALIZED IN FAUX FINISH WORK, "TRANSFORMING" THE INEXPENSIVE LUMBER USED TO TRIM THE HOME'S INTERIOR INTO RICH WOOD GRAINS AND FINE MARBLE.

In 1996, Jackson became the only city outside Russia ever to display the priceless treasures of St. Petersburg's golden age. More than 550,000 visitors flocked to the Mississippi Arts Pavilion to view *Palaces of St. Petersburg: Russian Imperial Style.*

THE GOOD LIFE

GIL FORD PHOTOGRAPHY, INC.

ENRIQUE ESPINOSA

JACKSON IS A CITY OF NEIGHBORHOODS, EACH WITH A PERSONALITY ALL ITS OWN. DEPENDING ON WHOM YOU ASK, "HOME" MAY MEAN A WELCOMING FRONT PORCH, A WATERFRONT VIEW, A STATELY SOUTHERN MANOR, OR A CONTEMPORARY MASTERPIECE.

JACKSON'S LONG, SULTRY SUMMERS AND
MILD WINTERS MAKE GARDENING A FA-
VORITE PASTIME AND ALFRESCO DINING
VIRTUALLY MANDATORY.

▲ TOM ROSTER

Once summer sets in, you'll find gardens bursting with colorful produce all over Jackson. But for those lacking a green thumb, the farmer's market on Woodrow Wilson Avenue is well-stocked with fresh-picked fruits and vegetables of every taste, color, and description.

JUST OUTSIDE JACKSON, THE CITYSCAPE
QUICKLY GIVES WAY TO RURAL MISSIS-
SIPPI, MARKED BY PASTORAL LANDSCAPES
AND A LEISURELY PACE THAT SEEM FAR
REMOVED FROM THE HUSTLE AND BUSTLE
OF THE CAPITAL CITY.

Old trucks and tough luck: Life in
the fast lane just isn't for everyone.

KNOWING THAT MISSISSIPPI HAS PRO-
DUCED MORE WRITERS PER SQUARE MILE
THAN ANY OTHER STATE, LOCALS ARE
FOND OF SAYING, "WE MAY NOT BE ABLE
TO READ, BUT WE SURE CAN WRITE."
HERE, JACKSON'S OWN WILLIE MORRIS,
AUTHOR OF THE AUTOBIOGRAPHICAL
WORKS *Good Old Boy* AND *My Dog Skip*,
PAYS HIS RESPECTS TO ANOTHER GREAT
MISSISSIPPI WRITER, WILLIAM FAULKNER.

PULITZER PRIZE WINNER EUDORA WELTY
HAS MADE JACKSON AND MISSISSIPPI
PROMINENT SETTINGS IN MANY OF HER
NOVELS. BEFORE SHE REACHED HER
TEENS, WELTY HAD ALREADY PUBLISHED
SEVERAL PIECES IN CHILDREN'S MAGA-
ZINES, AND SHE CONTINUED TO WRITE
STORIES WELL INTO HER SEVENTIES.

KING COTTON REIGNS SUPREME OVER
HUNDREDS OF ACRES OF FARMLAND JUST
OUTSIDE THE METRO AREA. AFTER THE
HARVEST EACH AUTUMN, TRUCKS LOADED
WITH THE FLUFFY STUFF ARE A COMMON
SIGHT ON LOCAL HIGHWAYS, AND LEFT-
OVER STRANDS FLOAT LAZILY IN THE WEL-
COME BREEZE.

WITH ITS OWN SUGAR AND SAW MILLS,
A COTTON GIN, A BLACKSMITH SHOP,
A SERVICE STATION, A TOWN JAIL, AND
MORE, THE AG MUSEUM CELEBRATES
MISSISSIPPI'S AGRARIAN HERITAGE
THROUGH REVEALING DEMONSTRATIONS
OF LIFE IN A 1920S FARMING TOWN.
THE ON-SITE EXHIBITION HALL HOUSES
DOZENS OF DETAILED EXHIBITS, MANY
OF WHICH STAR TALKING, SNORING
MANNEQUINS SO LIFELIKE THEY'VE BEEN
KNOWN TO MAKE UNSUSPECTING
VISITORS JUMP.

At various local events, city slickers are given plenty of chances to meet the animals face to face. Each fall at the State Fair (right), farmers from across Mississippi bring their finest specimens to vie for top honors— and maybe make a friend or two. In February, the Dixie National Rodeo (opposite) showcases its own litany of livestock, plus all the ropin' and ridin' a cowboy could ask for.

THE GOOD LIFE

WHETHER IT'S A LEISURELY JAUNT ON A
CRISP AUTUMN AFTERNOON, A FRIENDLY
GAME OF POLO, OR A HEATED JUMPING
COMPETITION AT THE FAIRGROUNDS,
HORSEBACK RIDING IS A POPULAR SPORT
IN JACKSON.

In 1998, Jackson hosted *Splendors of Versailles*, the largest exhibit ever presented highlighting France's most famous château. The exposition included more than 150 sculptures, paintings, furnishings, jewels, and other treasures, but the focal point was a specially commissioned, 10-ton, 12-foot replica of Gian Lorenzo Bernini's equestrian statue of Louis XIV.

Since its curtain rose for the first time in 1965, Jackson's New Stage Theatre has produced hundreds of classic plays and hosted a number of traveling shows from across the United States and abroad.

J.D. SCHWALM

DUBBED THE "OLYMPICS OF DANCE," THE USA INTERNATIONAL BALLET COMPETITION LURES CONTESTANTS AND SPECTATORS FROM AROUND THE WORLD EVERY FOUR YEARS. THE EVENT IS HELD AT THALIA MARA HALL (OPPOSITE), NAMED IN HONOR OF BALLET MISSISSIPPI'S FOUNDER, WHO IS CREDITED WITH BRINGING THE PRESTIGIOUS COMPETITION TO THE CAPITAL CITY.

JIMMY WINSTEAD

HOME TO A NUMBER OF WELL-REGARDED INSTITUTIONS OF HIGHER LEARNING, JACKSON IS COMMITTED TO EDUCATING YOUNG MINDS AND TRAINING A QUALIFIED WORKFORCE. MISSISSIPPI'S ONLY URBAN UNIVERSITY, JACKSON STATE UNIVERSITY HAS BEEN PROVIDING STUDENTS WITH A WELL-ROUNDED ACADEMIC EXPERIENCE SINCE 1877 (LEFT). FOUNDED IN 1883, BELHAVEN COLLEGE OFFERS A FOUR-YEAR LIBERAL ARTS AND SCIENCES EDUCATION IN THE PRESBYTERIAN TRADITION (RIGHT). AND MILLSAPS COLLEGE, ESTABLISHED BY THE METHODIST CHURCH IN 1890, IS AMONG THE NATION'S FINEST LIBERAL ARTS SCHOOLS, CONSISTENTLY EARNING KUDOS FROM *U.S. News & World Report* AND *National Review* (OPPOSITE).

More than 400 houses of worship serve virtually every faith and denomination in Jackson. Whether it's an intimate congregation with fewer than 100 members or a larger parish that numbers in the thousands, most people agree that attending church in Jackson is "a nice thing."

JACKSON

Locals are always searching for ways to glimpse the heavens, and thanks to the historic James Observatory at Millsaps College (opposite), stargazers can bring the universe within reach.

FROM T-SHIRTS AND TIES TO SEQUINS AND
SMILES, LOCALS AREN'T SHY ABOUT SUP-
PORTING THE HOME TEAM, WHETHER IT'S
A MINOR-LEAGUE BASEBALL GAME AT
SMITH-WILLS STADIUM (TOP) OR THE
FOOTBALL RIVALRY BETWEEN JACKSON
STATE UNIVERSITY AND MISSISSIPPI
VALLEY STATE UNIVERSITY (BOTTOM).

A Class AA professional team and farm club for the Houston Astros, the Jackson Generals have been hitting the diamond since 1975. Although the team is slated to relocate in the year 2000, minor-league baseball has proved to be an important economic force in the capital city, pumping more than $3 million a year into the local economy.

THE MISSISSIPPI SPORTS HALL OF FAME & MUSEUM IN JACKSON IS A HIGH-TECH, INTERACTIVE TRIBUTE TO THE STATE'S ATHLETIC HERITAGE. TOUCH-SCREEN KIOSKS ALLOW VISITORS TO VIEW ARCHIVAL FOOTAGE, BIOGRAPHICAL INFORMATION, AND MORE THAN 500 INTERVIEWS WITH FAMOUS MISSISSIPPI ATHLETES, INCLUDING JERRY RICE, ARCHIE MANNING, AND BRETT FAVRE.

A LOVE FOR SPORTS BEGINS EARLY IN
JACKSON, WHERE LOCALS WHO WOULD
RATHER PLAY THAN WATCH CAN JOIN IN
THE FUN WITH ONE OF THE CAPITAL
CITY'S YOUTH ATHLETIC LEAGUES.

JACKSON

THERE'S NO SHORTAGE OF WIDE-OPEN
SPACES IN AND AROUND JACKSON, WHERE
VERDANT FIELDS AND RUSTIC SWIMMING
HOLES INVITE EVERY RESIDENT TO TAKE
ADVANTAGE OF THE GREAT OUTDOORS.

▼ TOM ROSTER

MISSISSIPPI'S PRIME LOCATION FOR BASS FISHING, THE 33,000-ACRE ROSS BARNETT RESERVOIR ATTRACTS THOUSANDS OF SPORT FISHERMEN EACH SUMMER AND HOSTS A HANDFUL OF BIG-MONEY TOUR-NAMENTS. OF COURSE, THERE'S MUCH MORE TO THE "REZ" THAN BASS. THE WA-TERS JUST BELOW THE SPILLWAY ARE ALSO POPULATED BY PLENTY OF MONSTROUS CATFISH.

JACKSON

THE ROSS BARNETT RESERVOIR IS A HOT
SPOT FOR POWER BOATING, WATERSKIING,
SAILING, AND SWIMMING (WATCH OUT FOR
THOSE JET SKIS!). SURROUNDED BY MILES
OF WOODED COASTLINE DOTTED WITH
CAMPGROUNDS AND PICNIC AREAS, THE
REZ IS ALSO A MECCA FOR LANDLUBBERS
WHO CRAVE A TASTE OF THE GREAT
OUTDOORS.

While the capital city may not be known as a sailor's paradise, the Jackson Yacht Club stages multiclass regattas under sunny skies year-round (pages 148 and 149).

Music lovers gather on land and on water for the Mississippi Symphony Orchestra's Pepsi Pops concert at the Reservoir's Old Trace Park (top and opposite). Miles of quiet shoreline also make the Rez an ideal place to get away from it all (bottom).

Jackson's largest annual festival, Jubilee!JAM is a three-day celebration of art, music, food, and fun. Held every year since 1986, the event packs downtown with local and national entertainment, arts and crafts displays, children's activities, and food vendors cooking up everything from fresh alligator to fried zucchini.

FESTIVAL OR FAMILY REUNION, THE FOCAL
POINT OF ANY OUTDOOR GATHERING IN
JACKSON IS USUALLY FOOD, AND THE TAN-
TALIZING AROMAS OF CHICKEN, CRAWFISH,
BARBECUE, AND BURGERS ALWAYS SIGNAL
A GREAT AFTERNOON IN STORE.

HELD EACH MAY AND OCTOBER, THE CANTON FLEA MARKET ATTRACTS SOME 800 VENDORS FROM NEARLY 30 STATES AND THOUSANDS OF SHOPPERS FROM AROUND THE COUNTRY (LEFT AND OPPO-SITE TOP). WARES INCLUDE FINE ART, PAINTINGS, POTTERY, JEWELRY, CRAFTS, ANTIQUES, AND PLANTS. COME PREPARED TO FIGHT THE TRAFFIC AND DON'T FORGET YOUR FLASHLIGHT; THE BEST DEALS ARE OFTEN MADE BEFORE DAWN.

ALSO IN OCTOBER, MADISON'S HIS-TORIC CHAPEL OF THE CROSS HOSTS A DAY IN THE COUNTRY, AN ANNUAL FESTI-VAL AND CRAFTS FAIR FEATURING LIVE ENTERTAINMENT, CHILDREN'S ACTIVITIES, AND TOURS OF THE ANTEBELLUM CHURCH (OPPOSITE BOTTOM).

The Mississippi State Fair signals the arrival of fall in Jackson, with food, livestock shows, food, nationally renowned entertainment, food, and a midway packed with carnival rides, games, and, you guessed it, more food.

One of the largest events of its kind in the South, the 12-day Mississippi State Fair has put a unique spin on family fun and entertainment since the 1860s.

People have referred to Jackson as a "little Atlanta" or a "little Dallas," but in reality, Mississippi's capital is a dynamic, growing city all its own. We're equal parts valued tradition and visionary ideas. We're urban and rural, Old South and New. Truly, to live in Jackson is to know the good life.

Profiles in Excellence

A look at the corporations, businesses, professional groups, and community service organizations that have made this book possible. Their stories—offering an informal chronicle of the local business community—are arranged according to the date they were established in Jackson.

Baker, Donelson, Bearman & Caldwell

Barksdale Bonding & Insurance ◆ BellSouth ◆ Blue Cross & Blue Shield of Mississippi

Brown's Fine Art & Framing, Inc. ◆ Brunini, Grantham, Grower & Hewes, PLLC

Byrd & Associates ◆ Canizaro Trigiani Architects ◆ ChemFirst Inc. ◆ CommuniGroup

Deposit Guaranty National Bank ◆ The Edison Walthall Hotel ◆ Entergy Corporation

Friede Goldman International Inc. ◆ Harris Constructors, Inc. ◆ Hinds Community College

Horne CPA Group ◆ Jackson Academy ◆ Jitney Jungle Stores of America, Inc.

J.W. Underwood & Company ◆ Key Constructors, Inc. ◆ KLLM Transport Services, Inc.

Lextron Corporation ◆ LTM Enterprises, Inc./McDonald's ◆ Mattiace Properties, Inc.

Methodist Healthcare ◆ MetroJackson Chamber of Commerce ◆ Millsaps College

Mississippi Baptist Health Systems, Inc. ◆ Mississippi Blood Services ◆ Mississippi Business Journal

Mississippi Managed Care Network, Inc. ◆ Mississippi Valley Gas Company ◆ Nick's ◆ Northpark Mall

OffiSource ◆ Parkway Properties, Inc. ◆ River Oaks Health System ◆ Ross & Yerger

St. Dominic Health Services, Inc. ◆ Stuart C. Irby Company and Irby Construction Company

Trustmark National Bank ◆ Union Planters Bank ◆ U.S. Office Products

ValuePage ◆ Vickers, Incorporated ◆ Waste Management of Mississippi-Jackson

Watkins & Eager PLLC ◆ Watkins Ludlam Winter & Stennis, P.A.

WLBT-TV ◆ WorldCom

1860 - 1958

1860 Ross & Yerger

1880 MetroJackson Chamber of Commerce

1882 BellSouth

1889 Trustmark National Bank

1890 Millsaps College

1895 Watkins & Eager PLLC

1905 Watkins Ludlam Winter & Stennis, P.A.

1911 Mississippi Baptist Health Systems, Inc.

1917 Hinds Community College

1919 U.S. Office Products

1919 Jitney Jungle Stores of America, Inc.

1923 Entergy Corporation

1925 Deposit Guaranty National Bank

1926 Stuart C. Irby Company and Irby Construction Company

1928 The Edison Walthall Hotel

1928 OffiSource

1933 Barksdale Bonding & Insurance

1938 Canizaro Trigiani Architects

1946 Brunini, Grantham, Grower & Hewes, PLLC

1946 St. Dominic Health Services, Inc.

1947 Blue Cross & Blue Shield of Mississippi

1948 J.W. Underwood & Company

1951 Mississippi Valley Gas Company

1953 WLBT-TV

1956 Vickers, Incorporated

1957 ChemFirst Inc.

IN ONE OF LIFE'S IRONIES, MISSISSIPPI'S OLDEST INSURANCE AGENCY TRACES ITS beginnings to a disaster. If a blaze hadn't destroyed the mercantile firm of Ross, Yerger, & Co. in 1892, Ross & Yerger might have become Mississippi's most famous department store instead of one of the state's largest and most respected insurance agencies. ✳ In the late 1800s, three young businessmen—James Sively, James Ross, and Edward Yerger—signed an agreement establishing a

mercantile firm "to engage in the business of selling house furnishing goods and other merchandise."

Ross and Yerger quickly bought Sively's share of Ross, Yerger, & Co., and were soon reaping the benefits of a booming business built on impressive sales of willowware china. But just as the profits were reaching their peak, the mercantile establishment was destroyed by fire.

The company's insurance policy was with the firm of Barrows & Smythe, established in Jackson in 1860 and the first full-time insurance agency

in Mississippi. Barrows & Smythe paid the Ross, Yerger, & Co. claim quickly; in fact, the two young merchants were so impressed with the service, they bought the insurance firm, changing its name to Ross & Yerger.

Nine years later, Yerger bought out his partner and assumed sole ownership of the firm. A direct descendant of Yerger's has headed the company ever since.

"All of our employees have an understanding and appreciation of the history and heritage behind Ross & Yerger," says President Frank M. Yerger, the fourth generation of the Yerger family to lead the firm. "Throughout the company's history, we've held the same values as the original founders: integrity and honesty in our business relationships and a commitment to our clients that sets Ross & Yerger apart from the competition."

THE EXPERTS IN RISK MANAGEMENT

Today, Ross & Yerger has offices in Jackson and Tupelo. The firm provides individuals and businesses a range of services that include everything from auto and home owners'

coverage to property and casualty, workers' compensation, surety bonds, life insurance and employee benefit packages.

But while its diverse list of product offerings is a strength, Ross & Yerger's true point of difference is the expertise of its staff. Ross & Yerger recruits the top experts in risk management and employee benefits. The Ross & Yerger staff includes professionals who have attained the highest accreditations in the industry, earned only after rigorous study and outstanding performance in the field.

Ross & Yerger clients rely on the firm's experienced staff to develop unexpected alternatives that other insurance firms might miss. Instead of simply selling policies off the shelf, the Ross & Yerger experts look for new ways to treat risk—even if insurance is only one of the alternatives. This creative approach makes a difference for Ross & Yerger clients, both in their level of protection and in their bottom lines.

CLIENTS IN EVERY INDUSTRY

Ross & Yerger's impressive client list includes individuals and businesses in virtually every field. The region's most successful wholesalers, manufacturers, contractors, financial institutions, retailers, communications firms, public entities, health care providers, and associations trust their risk management programs to Ross & Yerger.

"Our record for retaining clients isn't based solely on providing coverage at a competitive premium," says Executive Vice President Eason Leake, who has been with Ross & Yerger since 1974. "Instead, we continuously evaluate our clients' programs to look for new needs and new opportunities. That means we have to know our

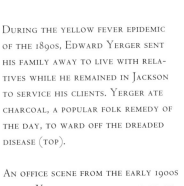

DURING THE YELLOW FEVER EPIDEMIC OF THE 1890S, EDWARD YERGER SENT HIS FAMILY AWAY TO LIVE WITH RELATIVES WHILE HE REMAINED IN JACKSON TO SERVICE HIS CLIENTS. YERGER ATE CHARCOAL, A POPULAR FOLK REMEDY OF THE DAY, TO WARD OFF THE DREADED DISEASE (TOP).

AN OFFICE SCENE FROM THE EARLY 1900S SHOWS YERGER AND HIS STAFF HARD AT WORK. A TYPICAL HOME OWNERS' POLICY OF THE DAY CARRIED A FACE VALUE OF $200 AND AN ANNUAL PREMIUM OF $5 (BOTTOM).

clients' businesses almost as well as they do. Ross & Yerger has an expert on staff to handle virtually any client need in any industry."

Ross & Yerger employs specialists in banking and finance, communications, construction, health care, oil and gas, medical malpractice, employee benefits, directors' and officers' liability, professional liability, and a number of other specialty areas. Every customized insurance plan is developed by a Ross & Yerger professional who understands the client.

COMMITMENT TO THE COMMUNITY

Ross & Yerger has historically been a major supporter of civic and cultural events in Jackson and Tupelo, and of community development efforts statewide.

The firm invests its time and resources in a number of charitable and civic organizations, including the MetroJackson Chamber of Commerce, Mississippi Museum of Art, United Way of the Capital Area, United Way of Greater Lee County, Community Development Foundation in Tupelo, Gateway Rescue Mission, Habitat for Humanity, Mississippi Economic Council, and many others.

Ross & Yerger's principals have also taken a personal interest in enhancing Mississippi0's quality of life, serving on the board of directors of the Mississippi Symphony Orchestra, Boys and Girls Clubs of Metropolitan Jackson, Improve Mis-

sissippi Political Action Committee (IMPAC), Capital Center Incorporated, Fondren-North Renaissance, Boy Scouts of America, Metropolitan Crime Commission, and Metropolitan YMCA.

Since 1860, Ross & Yerger has been a reliable source of the same superior service that originally inspired James Ross and Edward Yerger to join the insurance business. In a field in which stability and continuity of

coverage are critical, Ross & Yerger's longevity and outstanding record of service place the firm among the leading insurance agencies not only in Mississippi, but nationwide.

This exceptional service to both its clients and the community has been the driving force behind Ross & Yerger for more than a century, and will continue to be a Ross & Yerger hallmark well into the next millennium.

CLOCKWISE FROM TOP LEFT: ROSS & YERGER EMPLOYS THE TOP EXPERTS IN RISK MANAGEMENT AND EMPLOYEE BENEFITS. CLIENTS RELY ON THE FIRM'S EXPERIENCED STAFF TO DEVELOP CREATIVE SOLUTIONS TO THEIR INSURANCE NEEDS.

OUTSTANDING CLIENT SERVICE HAS SET ROSS & YERGER APART FOR MORE THAN A CENTURY.

TODAY, ROSS & YERGER IS LED BY CHAIRMAN OF THE BOARD WIRT YERGER JR. AND HIS SON, PRESIDENT FRANK M. YERGER. THE YERGERS ARE AMONG JACKSON'S MOST RESPECTED BUSINESS AND COMMUNITY LEADERS.

MetroJackson Chamber of Commerce

THE REVITALIZATION OF THE OLD CENTRAL FIRE STATION, WHERE THE MetroJackson Chamber of Commerce currently resides, serves to reflect the role the Chamber plays in its home community today. Built in 1904 as the main fire station for the City of Jackson, the building was vacant for many years until a group of area businessmen came together in 1977 to preserve the downtown landmark. ✳ Likewise, the Chamber itself has worked since its

founding in 1880 to create avenues for local businesses to combine their strengths. This, in turn, has produced a thriving economic environment in the tricounty metro area. Some of the nation's strongest industry leaders have emerged from this nurturing climate—particularly in the telecommunications and health care fields—and their success has attracted both national and global interest in the Metro Jackson area. By helping each other through the Chamber, these businesses have helped make Metro Jackson a major economic destination.

The Chamber was originally known as the Jackson Board of Trade and was later incorporated as the Jackson Chamber of Commerce in 1933. The most significant transition in its history occurred in 1992 when it became the MetroJackson Chamber of Commerce. This was much more than a name change; it introduced a major shift in focus, stretching beyond the Jackson city limits to invite businesses in Hinds, Madison, and Rankin

SINCE ITS FOUNDING IN 1880, THE METROJACKSON CHAMBER OF COMMERCE HAS WORKED TO BUILD A THRIVING ECONOMY IN THE TRICOUNTY AREA (TOP).

LOCATED IN THE HEART OF MISSISSIPPI'S CAPITOL CITY, THE METROJACKSON CHAMBER OF COMMERCE CONTRIBUTES TO REGIONAL GROWTH BY STIMULATING ECONOMIC TRAFFIC BOTH WITHIN THE TRICOUNTY AREA—WHICH COVERS A POPULATION BASE OF MORE THAN 450,000—AND BEYOND ITS BORDERS (BOTTOM).

counties to join the Chamber's membership. Through this expansion, the Chamber contributed to growth in the broader region by stimulating economic traffic both within the tricounty area—which covers a population base of more than 450,000—and beyond its borders. Current MetroJackson Chamber President Duane O'Neill says, "Ten other chambers exist within the three counties that make up our metro community, and each focuses on the special needs of its particular area. The MetroJackson Chamber focuses on strengthening the entire metro area as a whole. Creating the metro concept from an economic development and regional marketing perspective is a key effort of the MetroJackson Chamber."

STIMULATING THE REGIONAL ECONOMY

Taking the metro concept a step further, the Chamber spearheaded formation of the Metro Economic Development Alliance (MEDA) in 1994. O'Neill says, "There are economic development authorities or dis-

tricts for each of the three counties that try to attract business from outside of the region. They are Hinds County Economic Development District, Rankin First, and Madison County Economic Development Authority. These three joined forces with the Jackson International Airport and the MetroJackson Chamber to form this alliance." MEDA primarily coordinates the marketing and economic development efforts in the tricounty area.

By hosting regional events with a business focus, the Chamber has created additional opportunities for area companies to learn more about their fellow Chamber members. Twice annually, the Chamber sponsors Prospecting in the P.M., a small-business trade show that sells out regularly each summer and fall. Through Prospecting and other networking events, Chamber members are able to gain broader exposure for their businesses and the products and services they offer. In addition, the Chamber recognizes top businesses (from both the large and small sectors) in the metro community each spring with the annual Business & Industry Super Achievers Awards Luncheon.

Small-business development is another key activity of the Metro-Jackson Chamber. The Small Business Council sponsors numerous seminars throughout the year on issues relating to small, growing local enterprises. ChamberPlus, Inc., a health benefits program formed through a partnership between the Chamber and Blue Cross & Blue Shield of Mississippi, allows companies employing between two and 50 people the same purchasing options for employee health care benefits that larger companies enjoy. "Often, small businesses—and most chambers are made up of small businesses—lack the ability to obtain health care benefits, let alone at a rate that is acceptable," says current Chamber Chairman of the Board LeRoy Walker. "By pooling the entire Chamber membership together, we've been able to make such benefits not only obtainable, but affordable."

WORKING TO IMPROVE THE ENTIRE COMMUNITY

Through a broad array of programs, subcommittees, and strategic initiatives, the MetroJackson Chamber participates in many nontraditional Chamber activities. The organization encourages public involvement in crime prevention by facilitating MetroJackson Crime Stoppers—with a special 24-hour hot line for citizens to report information relating to specific crimes—and special judicial system meetings. The Chamber also has initiated a proactive program aimed at keeping teens away from crime. One-to-One: MetroJackson Mentoring Partnership works with 61 provider groups throughout the tri-county area whose efforts already focus on providing positive, supportive environments for children. One-to-One focuses on providing mentors from the business community to work with individual children who are in need of a mentor and role model. Judge Pat Wise, cochair of the One-to-One effort, says that One-to-One was organized because business leaders saw a need to reach young people before

they are drawn into possible criminal activities.

Because fostering a positive business environment typically includes legislative issues, the Chamber is involved in governmental relations. Through a number of subcommittees, members learn about issues affecting their businesses and voice concerns to appropriate legislative representatives at the local, state, and national levels. Each January, the Chamber holds one of Mississippi's largest receptions for state legislators.

The Chamber works to foster a strong labor pool through training and workforce development initiatives in education. Public Recognition of Improvement and Dedication in Education (P.R.I.D.E.) and Business/Industry/Teacher Exchange (BITE) are examples of the Chamber's efforts to participate in improving education in area schools. In addition, the Chamber recognizes outstanding teachers throughout the metro community through its annual Metro Teacher Recognition Luncheon.

Improving race relations is also part of the Chamber's efforts to embrace diversity within the community and to address issues that impede progress. Leadership Jackson, now entering its 12th year, has received recognition from the National Association for Community Leadership for several years. The program strives to educate participants on major issues and alternative approaches to

solving community problems. Leadership Jackson enrolls 40 participants each year and has a current alumni base of 360 local business leaders.

Through diverse programs aimed at improving the regional economy, the MetroJackson Chamber of Commerce has helped the area become a better place to live and work. "We want to be able to give our members something in addition to the intangibles of taking care of the business climate and making sure that we make this a great place to do business, bring in more jobs, and help train a workforce," says O'Neill. "Doing other community-building things that directly affect the bottom line for businesses is where our efforts will continue in the future."

ORIGINALLY KNOWN AS THE JACKSON BOARD OF TRADE AND LATER INCORPORATED AS THE JACKSON CHAMBER OF COMMERCE IN 1933, THE METROJACKSON CHAMBER OF COMMERCE ADOPTED ITS CURRENT NAME IN 1992.

THE METRO JACKSON AREA CONTINUES TO EXHIBIT STRONG LEADERSHIP IN THE HEALTH CARE INDUSTRY.

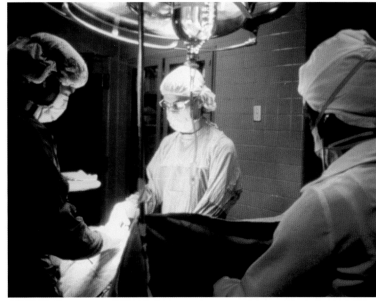

BELLSOUTH

MISSISSIPPI'S PRIMARY LOCAL TELEPHONE SERVICE PROVIDER, BELLSOUTH, IS both a pioneer and a modern-day leader in the telecommunications industry. Headquartered in Atlanta, BellSouth operates in nine states, including North Carolina, South Carolina, Georgia, Kentucky, Louisiana, Florida, Alabama, Tennessee, and Mississippi. ✳ Based in Jackson, BellSouth-Mississippi services more than 1.2 million access lines throughout

the state. The company provides telephone service and data links for wire transmissions—modems, fax machines, and computers—in 81 of Mississippi's 82 counties. BellSouth continues to expand its technologically advanced network, working to become a one-stop provider of telecommunications services for Mississippi customers.

A TECHNOLOGICAL LEADER

Ever since Jackson's first telephone was installed in the mayor's office in 1882, the company that would eventually be known as BellSouth has worked to provide a reliable communications

system for every residence and business in Mississippi. The company is committed to maintaining its position as a telecommunications leader, introducing new technologies as soon as they become available.

BellSouth's state-of-the-art network is second to none. The company has invested approximately $3 billion in Mississippi's telecommunications infrastructure, including fiber optics, digital connectivity, and Integrated Services Digital Network (ISDN) lines.

Fiber-optic cable allows fast, error-free transmission of high-tech signals. Made of hair-thin glass filaments, fiber optics transmit large amounts of data—including voice, video, and computer signals—at the speed of light.

Mississippi has more than 92,000 miles of fiber-optic cable in place, with more being put into the ground every day. The state's fiber-optic mileage relative to population

density is among the highest in the nation. BellSouth also pioneered the Mississippi FiberNet 2000 project, the nation's first fiber-optic-based, fully digital, and interactive two-way distance learning network.

BellSouth was among the first to offer ISDN, the technology that allows the integration of voice and data signals over a single telephone

GIL FORD PHOTOGRAPHY

GIL FORD PHOTOGRAPHY

GIL FORD PHOTOGRAPHY

BELLSOUTH, HEADQUARTERED IN THE LANDMARK CENTER ON CAPITOL STREET (BOTTOM), PROVIDES STATE-OF-THE-ART TELECOMMUNICATIONS SERVICES THROUGHOUT MISSISSIPPI. FROM SUCH HIGH-TECH SERVICES AS LOCAL- AND WIDE-AREA NETWORK CONFIGURATIONS (TOP LEFT) TO HIGH-SPEED INTERNET ACCESS (TOP RIGHT), BELLSOUTH IS EQUIPPED TO PROVIDE ITS CUSTOMERS WITH THE LATEST TELECOMMUNICATIONS SERVICES.

line. ISDN makes videoconferencing, PC-to-PC file transfer, and long-distance medical imaging possible.

BellSouth continually unveils new technologies for home and business communications. Recent innovations include SmartRing, ZipConnect, and a high-speed broadband network. SmartRing is a rerouting service that provides an alternate path when the primary route is interrupted by broken or damaged cable. SmartRing is an innovative network design that utilizes fiber-optic facilities in a ring topology.

ZipConnect allows callers to dial a single number for a multilocation business and become automatically connected to the office nearest the caller's zip code. This technology saves time that would otherwise be spent poring through multiple listings in a telephone book.

BellSouth's sophisticated Asynchronous Transfer Mode-Synchronous Optical Network Transmission (ATM-SONET) high-speed broadband network offers business customers two-way interactive video services for distance learning, videoconferencing, and high-resolution medical imaging. The broadband service is an integral part of the Mississippi Information

Superhighway, which is designed to connect schools, universities, community colleges, hospitals, and other public sites.

In 1997, BellSouth's National Directory Assistance Center established operations in Jackson. When callers dial 1+411, they are asked for the state and city of the party whose number they need. Callers no longer have to remember to dial one number for local directory assistance and another for long-distance directory assistance. BellSouth offers both local and nationwide listings from a single telephone number—1+411.

CUSTOMER-FRIENDLY SOLUTIONS

BellSouth is customer focused, creating products and services that make advanced communications easy to use, and was the first telephone company to establish 24-hour customer service. National studies conducted by J.D. Power and Associates ranked BellSouth as the leader in customer satisfaction twice among the largest telephone companies.

In addition to superior customer service, BellSouth-Mississippi stresses community involvement. The company supports a number of charitable causes and donates its employees' time and expertise to specific telecommunications-related projects, including wiring Mississippi schools for Internet access.

"Telephone service is an integral part of people's lives at home and at work," says J. Kelly Allgood, BellSouth president-Mississippi. "BellSouth is proud to operate the most reliable network available at the most affordable rates. In Jackson and in Mississippi, BellSouth is the telecommunications provider."

THE INTEGRATED SERVICES DIGITAL NETWORK (ISDN) PROVIDES THE INFRASTRUCTURE BACKBONE TO SUPPORT SUCH DISTANCE-LEARNING APPLICATIONS AS THIS MULTIMEDIA CLASSROOM.

▶ GIL FORD PHOTOGRAPHY

A STRONG CUSTOMER FOCUS HAS LED BELLSOUTH TO RECEIVE THE HIGHEST RATING FOR CUSTOMER SERVICE IN SEVERAL NATIONAL SURVEYS, INCLUDING J.D. POWER. BY CONCENTRATING ON CUSTOMER NEEDS, BELLSOUTH HAS BEEN ABLE TO EARN A REPUTATION OF PUTTING THE CUSTOMER FIRST.

I'S ONLY FITTING THAT THE BANK EVENTUALLY KNOWN AS TRUSTMARK WAS THE SOLE financial institution in Jackson that did not close its doors during the government-ordered "bank holiday" of the Great Depression. ✳ "We were the only bank open the first four days in March of 1933 that paid 100 cents on the dollar," the bank's head teller later recalled. "We stayed open every day until every customer was served. Some people even brought their money back, thinking it wasn't safe at

home." For more than a century, this same level of confidence, integrity, and service—even in the toughest times—has been the hallmark of Trustmark National Bank.

Jackson's oldest financial institution, Trustmark has its origins in the founding of the Jackson Bank in 1889. Over the next nine decades, the original bank acquired and merged

with other financial institutions, operating under the names State National Bank, Jackson-State National Bank, and First National Bank.

In 1985, the bank adopted the name Trustmark and the credo "We earn your trust every day," an identity that reflects the bank's commitment to quality customer service and products. Operating under the original 1889

charter of the Jackson Bank, Trustmark continues to build on its legacy of dependability, integrity, and hard work to fulfill its vision to be a premier financial services company in its markets.

PURSUING OPPORTUNITIES FOR GROWTH

Trustmark operates more than 180 branches in 49 Mississippi communi-

ties, including 26 full-service branches in Jackson. The bank's total assets exceed $5 billion. Trustmark first turned its attention to markets outside the capital city in 1966, acquiring banks in Gloster, McComb, Tylertown, and Greenville. Trustmark continues to expand into new communities, both by establishing new banks and by acquiring existing financial institutions. It's a strategy that not only allows Trustmark to grow, but also benefits the customers, who often gain new financial services and an increased depth of talent when Trustmark comes to town.

"Mississippi has been good to Trustmark," says Harry M. Walker, Trustmark president and chief operating officer. "In turn, Trustmark looks for opportunities in locations that will mean growth for our bank, benefits for our customers, and increased value for our shareholders."

Trustmark's strategy for future growth includes plans to acquire other banks not only in Mississippi, but possibly desirable markets in contiguous states. Trustmark banks located near the state lines already attract customers from Alabama, Tennessee, Arkansas, and Louisiana.

High Tech with a Personal Touch

Trustmark is a technological leader, offering electronic and on-line banking, debit cards, automated teller machines, and all the other modern services customers expect from one of the state's largest financial institutions. But rather than touting technology as its strongest selling point, Trustmark focuses on the personal touch.

"Technology is merely a tool. Banking is about relationships, and relationships are always about people," says Walker. "Some of our customers may never use a computer or a debit card, and that's fine with us. Customers have to trust the bank to provide the service that's right for them, and

at Trustmark, that's what we do every day. We focus on our customers."

The personal touch extends to the local community served by Trustmark, where the bank works to improve the quality of life for everyone. As part of its mission to support the Jackson community, the bank reaches out to people in need through its sponsorship of the Trustmark Red Beans and Rice Festival, an annual fund-raiser for Stewpot Community Services in Jackson. In addition, Trustmark's Tour LeFleur Bicycle Race is a major fund-raising event for the Blair E. Batson Hospital for Children at the University of Mississippi Medical Center. The bank and its branches

sponsor parties, dances, and social events for nursing home residents, and participate in 31 Adopt-A-School programs statewide.

"Earning our customers' trust means more than just doing a good job within the walls of the bank," says Walker. "It means contributing to the communities where we operate, and touching as many people in those communities as we can—even those who never set foot inside a Trustmark lobby."

With Trustmark's long history of dependable service and steady growth, the bank will continue to be a valuable part of the Jackson community for many years to come.

TRUSTMARK IS A TECHNOLOGICAL LEADER, OFFERING ELECTRONIC AND ON-LINE BANKING, DEBIT CARDS, AUTOMATED TELLER MACHINES, AND ALL THE OTHER MODERN SERVICES CUSTOMERS EXPECT FROM ONE OF THE STATE'S LARGEST FINANCIAL INSTITUTIONS.

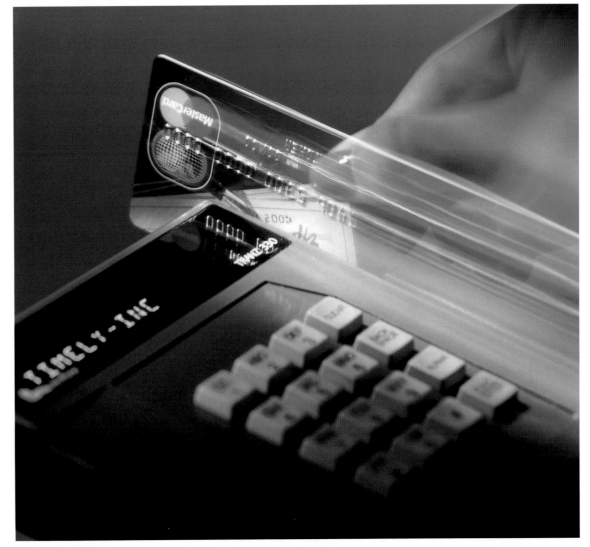

OUNDED IN 1890 AND AFFILIATED WITH THE UNITED METHODIST CHURCH, Millsaps College is a nationally respected, selective liberal arts college located in the heart of the capital city. Since its earliest days, the small college has played a large role in promoting its home city. The horse-and-buggy has long since given way to the automobile, but the principles of the college founders have remained constant. Millsaps exists to teach and teach well. For more than a century, the rolling

hills and oak-shaded hollows of the 100-acre campus have been home to a distinguished community of students and faculty united in their pursuit of excellence.

A visitor's casual glance toward the lush lawns beside Murrah Hall reveals freshmen circled around the massive M-bench, engaged in debate. Their professor quietly listens, letting tomorrow's leaders have their say. Barely visible through a sunlit window, two M.B.A. students sit in a study room, reviewing their case. Across the manicured campus, a Master of Liberal Studies student receives one-on-one instruction in a painting class. Slowly, a pattern emerges, and a truth comes to light. Millsaps is not merely a place scenic in nature, but a way of thinking, open and fertile.

A Place for Growth

Millsaps students matriculate from widely differing backgrounds with uniformly strong scholastic foundations. How strong? More than half of entering freshmen graduated in the top 10 percent of their respective

classes. For 1997, the average ACT was 27 and the average SAT, 1220. Representing 30 states and nine foreign countries, they come to Millsaps not to learn what to think, but to learn *how* to think.

Ninety-one percent of the full-time Millsaps faculty hold a doctorate or terminal degree. They are distinguished scholars and researchers with substantial reputations in their fields, and all subscribe to the proposition that a teacher's first responsibility is to teach well. With a student-faculty ratio of 13-to-1, and an average class

size of 16 students, Millsaps is the perfect atmosphere for intellectual exchange.

Millsaps' nationally acclaimed core curriculum enables students to make connections among fields of study and to integrate this knowledge in a holistic way. Through traditional majors and numerous preprofessional, interdisciplinary, and special programs, Millsaps offers innovative courses that stress critical thinking skills, analytical reasoning, and independence of thought.

The Millsaps graduate has the skills to compete—and excel—in the most demanding academic and professional arenas. More than 40 percent of undergraduates attend graduate or professional schools immediately after graduation. Historically, more than three-fourths of the law, medical, and dental school applicants from Millsaps are accepted into the program of their choice. Millsaps' state-of-the-art laboratories and classrooms have also produced four Rhodes Scholars.

Recognizing the importance of professional degree programs, Millsaps offers the Master of Business Admin-

CLOCKWISE FROM TOP:
A VIEW OF THE MILLSAPS TOWER (BACKGROUND) FROM THE BOWL—THE CENTRAL GATHERING PLACE ON CAMPUS—REVEALS THE STATE-OF-THE-ART OLIN HALL OF SCIENCE (LEFT).

THE MILLSAPS SECRET: LEARNING CAN BE FUN.

THE MASSIVE M-BENCH IS A POPULAR GATHERING PLACE FOR RELAXATION IN THE SUN AND FOR CLASS MEETINGS, TOO.

STEWART COHEN

istration and Master of Accountancy through the Else School of Management. An innovative curriculum, small classes, faculty-student interaction, and unique programs are just a few of the many reasons why tomorrow's business leaders seek out the distinguished Else School of Management.

A SENSE OF COMMUNITY

Millsaps' liberal arts foundation is designed to foster a sense of community among students and to inspire them to reach out into the wider community of their city, state, nation, and world. The college believes strongly in the importance of giving back and instills this principle of outreach through all classes.

Three-fourths of the student body lives on campus in residential facilities, and resident and commuter students alike are highly involved in extracurricular activities. The student community participates in service organizations such as Habitat for Humanity, puts on dramatic and musical productions, publishes a newspaper, yearbook, and literary magazine, maintains national social and service fraternities and sororities, and has an active student government.

The Millsaps-Wilson Library's 250,000-unit multimedia collection is accessible seven days a week, and computer labs provide Internet and library access. With photography darkrooms, rehearsal halls, research and language labs, a writing center, and other amenities, students have

valuable, available research centers no matter what their needs.

Millsaps fields six women's and seven men's varsity NCAA Division III sports teams, and student athletes have an impressive 97 percent graduation rate. Additionally, three-fourths of the student body participates in a comprehensive intramural program, and a planned student activities center will grant even more recreation opportunities.

A BEACON OF LEARNING

Millsaps is one of only four U.S. colleges to earn a chapter of the prestigious liberal arts honorary society Phi Beta Kappa, as well as professional accreditation of both its undergraduate and graduate business programs by the American Assembly of Collegiate Schools of Business-International Association for Management Educa-

tion. Millsaps also established the state's first Adult Degree Program in 1982. Taught by full-time faculty, this nationally recognized program offers regular classes on a more flexible basis for working adults.

U.S. News & World Report and *National Review* consistently rank Millsaps among the finest national liberal arts colleges, and *Barron's, Money, U.S. News & World Report*, and *The Fiske Guide to Colleges* consider Millsaps one of the best values in college education.

Millsaps has long been a treasure for the people of Jackson. The college brings internationally renowned speakers to the city and supports local cultural events. Positive influence and patronage have also flowed from the city to the college, and continue to do so. Jackson is a progressive, dynamic city, and Millsaps is proud to play a vital role in its continued advancement.

Watkins & Eager PLLC

Watkins & Eager's impressive legacy began in 1895, when William Hamilton "Will" Watkins became the 20th lawyer at the Jackson bar. Watkins' influential career spanned more than six decades and included more than 25 appearances before the U.S. Supreme Court. ✳ While Watkins' individual achievements were many, his most enduring contribution to the legal field in Mississippi was the founding of the law firm that bears his name today, more than a century since the young lawyer hung his first shingle on Capitol Street.

A Legal Legacy

Watkins teamed with Pat Eager to form Watkins & Eager in 1916. Eager never attended law school; instead, he persuaded Watkins to let him study the law in the firm's offices, working without pay until he passed the bar exam and won his first case. Eager practiced with the firm until his death in 1970, earning recognition as a premier trial lawyer and as the first Mississippi lawyer invited into the American College of Trial Lawyers.

The firm's reputation continued to flourish under the leadership and influence of two of Watkins' children. His son Tom earned a national reputation in the representation of corporate and governmental clients. In 1934, Elizabeth Watkins Hulen joined her father and brother in the firm. She became an outstanding appellate advocate and was the first woman from Mississippi to argue a case before the U.S. Supreme Court.

Will Watkins' grandson, William "Bill" Goodman, arrived at the firm in 1953, and has provided leadership throughout the second half of the century. The family tradition continued when Will Goodman, great-grandson of the firm's founder, joined the firm in 1977.

The Membership

Today, Watkins & Eager is a professional limited liability firm comprised of more than 50 members and associates. Individual members have been invited into membership in the nation's top legal organizations, including the American College of Trial Lawyers,

the American Academy of Appellate Lawyers, the Product Liability Advisory Council, the American College of Trust and Estate Counsel, and the American College of Employment Lawyers.

One of the firm's active members, Charles Clark, is the retired chief judge of the U.S. Court of Appeals for the Fifth Circuit. U.S. Senator Thad Cochran formerly practiced with the firm.

Many others have contributed to the growth and success of the firm's full-service, diversified law practice. As a result, professional publications throughout the 20th century have recognized Watkins & Eager as a leading law firm composed of preeminent lawyers. One example is the firm's selection for more than 50 consecutive years to author the annual digest of Mississippi law published by Martindale-Hubbell.

The Practice

Watkins & Eager has traditionally engaged in a general civil practice with an emphasis on litigation.

Today, the firm continues to enjoy both a broadscale trial practice in state and federal courts and before administrative agencies, and a comprehensive appellate practice at both the state and federal levels. The firm continues to expand upon its historic position as a leading litigation law firm in Mississippi.

The firm's practice encompasses nonlitigation matters as well. Today, Watkins & Eager is privileged to represent, among others, banking and financial institutions, manufacturers, oil and gas producers, telecommunications providers, investors, insurers, institutions of higher learning, and governmental agencies at the municipal, county, state, and federal levels.

Continuing the Tradition

Fortunate to have inherited a legacy of excellence, Watkins & Eager's goal is to continue to attract individuals to its ranks who have a keen intellect, logical reasoning power, and high ideals—men and women prepared for the demands that the 21st century will make upon the legal profession.

WATKINS & EAGER'S OFFICES ARE LOCATED IN THE HISTORIC EMPORIUM BUILDING AT 400 EAST CAPITOL STREET.

Jitney Jungle Stores of America, Inc.

I N 1919, W.H. Holman and W.B. McCarty opened a one-room grocery on Capitol Street in downtown Jackson. McCarty and Holman decided to call the store Jitney Jingle, playing off an advertising jingle that used the word "jitney," then slang for taxicab. But when a typographical error in a newspaper ad erroneously dubbed the store Jitney Jungle, the name stuck. ✳ That small store with the funny name has grown to become not only a Jackson institution, but one of

the largest grocery chains in the United States. Ranked by *Forbes* magazine as one of the largest private companies in the country, Jitney Jungle Stores of America, Inc. operates some 200 groceries and 60 gas stations in Mississippi, Alabama, Tennessee, Arkansas, Louisiana, and Florida. With annual sales topping $2 billion and more than 18,000 associates on the payroll, Jitney Jungle is one of Mississippi's largest retailers and private employers, and is the nation's 39th-largest grocery chain.

Innovations in Grocery Shopping

Jitney Jungle operates a number of grocery chains, each with its own distinct identity and each offering a different benefit to customers. Jitney Jungle stores are traditional, neighborhood groceries. Sack and Save stores and Megamarkets are large discount stores offering lower prices in a no-frills setting. The company's newest concept, Jitney Premier, made its debut in Jackson in 1994, and offers expanded services including pharmacies, video rentals, and gourmet and fresh food product lines in a pleasant setting.

Jitney Jungle's tremendous growth stems from an expansion program that includes building stores in new markets and acquiring chains in adjacent states. Major acquisitions in the 1980s and 1990s included Kroger stores in Alabama Megamarket stores in Memphis and Little Rock; the 28-store Foodway chain in Alabama, Tennessee, and Mississippi; the Louisiana-based Foodway chain; and the 118-store, Alabama-based Delchamps chain.

Committed to Mississippi

"We're proud of the growth our company has experienced throughout the South, but the accomplishment we're

most proud of is that Jitney has provided and continues to provide thousands of jobs here in Mississippi," says Henry Holman, chairman of the board. "Jitney is proof that Mississippi-based companies can and do succeed on a national level, primarily because of the dedication and support of a great base of employees and customers."

Jitney Jungle was owned by the Holman family until 1996, when the grocery chain underwent a $373 million leveraged buyout by Bruckman, Rosser, Sherrill & Co., a New York-based investment firm. The company's corporate headquarters and distribution centers, including eight warehouses

and a transportation center, remained in Jackson.

Jitney's commitment to Jackson reaches beyond employment to include charitable causes throughout the capital city. Jitney Jungle is a major supporter of the University of Mississippi Medical Center Children's Hospital, as well as a contributor to local schools and churches.

"We hope to continue growing and to become one of the largest grocery store chains not only in the South, but nationwide," Holman says. "But we plan to remain headquartered in Jackson, providing more and better jobs for Mississippians."

JACKSON MAYOR HARVEY JOHNSON (CENTER, WITH SCISSORS) CUT THE RIBBON TO OPEN A NEW JITNEY PREMIER IN JACKSON AS ONE OF HIS FIRST OFFICIAL DUTIES UPON TAKING OFFICE. TO JOHNSON'S LEFT IS JITNEY CHAIRMAN HENRY HOLMAN.

JITNEY'S FLAGSHIP STORE—THE FIRST JITNEY PREMIER TO OPEN, IN 1994—IS LOCATED ON OLD CANTON ROAD IN JACKSON.

MENTIONING THE WORDS "LAW FIRM" OFTEN BRINGS TO MIND IMAGES OF courtrooms and legal briefs. But when the firm in question is Watkins Ludlam Winter & Stennis, P.A., the picture may expand to include the Ross Barnett Reservoir, the revitalization of downtown Jackson, and nearly a century of community service. ✳ "There's more to being a lawyer than simply rendering service to clients," says John Hampton Stennis, a senior member

of the firm. "The role of the legal profession is also to provide vision, leadership, and ideas that lead to the betterment of the community. A commitment to public service is part of the oath we take when we enter the profession."

A LEGACY OF COMMUNITY SERVICE

In 1958, the city of Jackson was in need of a dependable water supply; Lakeland Drive ended at the Pearl River and few Jacksonians owned pleasure boats. When the Mississippi legislature passed a historic act calling for the creation of the 33,000-acre reservoir, Watkins Ludlam Winter & Stennis, P.A. did more than simply put together the project's necessary

financing package. Under the unifying leadership of Vaughan Watkins—then the firm's senior partner—the reservoir moved from a controversial "Jackson project" to a well-organized, five-county effort led by the Pearl River Valley Water Supply District. Watkins is also credited with having the foresight to include recreation as a major component of the reservoir's development plan.

Watkins Ludlam Winter & Stennis' commitment to the community was demonstrated again in the early 1960s when downtown Jackson was threatened with virtual extinction. Department stores, restaurants, and businesses were fleeing a deteriorating downtown in favor of the suburbs. Most of the storefronts along Capi-

tol Street were boarded up and sewage-filled Town Creek rushed through the middle of the business district, adding perpetual flooding to the city's list of problems.

Recognizing the desperate need for urban renewal, Watkins organized the Jackson Redevelopment Authority. Watkins Ludlam Winter & Stennis served as counsel for the organization, not only providing the vision and leadership that initiated the revitalization project, but also developing the creative financing and bond programs that paid for it. Under the firm's leadership, the organization literally rebuilt downtown Jackson. Dilapidated buildings were renovated or razed and replaced with modern structures and parking garages. Originally planned for the suburbs, the McCoy Federal Building was instead constructed downtown, providing an anchor for upscale developments and office space. Town Creek was diverted, and the impressive Deposit Guaranty Plaza and the Landmark Center were built on land once deemed unusable due to flooding.

Watkins Ludlam Winter & Stennis' history of community service is not limited to Jackson. The firm handled financing for the State Aid Road program, which linked isolated rural areas to Mississippi state highways. Watkins Ludlam Winter & Stennis, P.A. served as counsel in the issuance of Mississippi's first Industrial Development Revenue Bonds, which generated business growth statewide.

State and local officials continue to draw on Watkins Ludlam Winter & Stennis' experience in public finance. The first Mississippi law firm to become nationally recognized as a

"THERE IS MORE TO BEING A LAWYER THAN SIMPLY RENDERING SERVICE TO CLIENTS. THE ROLE OF THE LEGAL PROFESSIONAL IS ALSO TO PROVIDE VISION, LEADERSHIP, AND IDEAS THAT LEAD TO THE BETTERMENT OF THE COMMUNITY. A COMMITMENT TO PUBLIC SERVICE IS PART OF THE OATH WE TAKE WHEN WE ENTER THE PROFESSION," SAYS JOHN HAMPTON STENNIS.

municipal bond counsel, Watkins Ludlam Winter & Stennis, P.A. has handled many of Mississippi's municipal bond issues. The firm maintains the largest, most comprehensive bond practice in the state.

The firm is well known for its talent, having 50-plus attorneys who practice in many different areas of law. Graduates of law schools and universities nationwide, these attorneys bring to the firm their diverse abilities and backgrounds to serve client needs.

LEADERSHIP IN THE COMMUNITY

Community service has become a hallmark of the firm, and Watkins Ludlam Winter & Stennis, P.A. has provided leadership locally, regionally, and nationally. The firm mediated the development of the Madison County Public Schools, uniting parents and county school officials in a decision regarding where to locate new schools. Members of the firm organized the Metro Jackson Housing Partnership, an organization that rehabilitates substandard housing in downtown Jackson. Firm members also created the Foundation for the Mid South, which works to improve economic and social conditions in Arkansas, Mississippi, and Louisiana. The Enterprise Corporation of the Delta, a spin-off of the Foundation for the Mid South, provides venture capital for small-business start-ups in the region.

The Center for Non-Profits, which links nonprofit groups for economy in purchasing, was also a Watkins Ludlam Winter & Stennis concept. In addition, Watkins Ludlam Winter & Stennis is a member of the State Capital Law Firm Group, which includes 50 independent law firms— one from each state—in leadership positions in their respective states.

Members of the firm have served in the Mississippi House of Representatives and other positions of high public responsibility, including governor, lieutenant governor, and state treasurer of the state of Mississippi; chief counsel to the U.S. Senate Judiciary Committee; member of the Federal Power Commission; and chairs of the Southern Regional Education Board, Southern Growth Policies Board, Appalachian Regional Commission, and Commission on the Future of the South.

Lawyers at Watkins Ludlam Winter & Stennis, P.A. are active in the Mississippi Economic Council, Mississippi Manufacturers Association, Metro Jackson Chamber of Commerce, and Mississippi Water Resources Association, and are significantly involved in groups supporting the arts, the humanities, and civic responsibility.

"Obviously we're proud of the work we've done for our clients and of the cases we've won, but I think we're most proud of the cumulative effect of the firm's efforts in improving Mississippi," says William Winter, a senior member of the firm and former governor of Mississippi. "To see tangible evidence of the contributions our firm has made, and is still making today, all you have to do is drive around our state."

CLOCKWISE FROM TOP LEFT: ALVENO CASTILLA IS THE CHAIR OF THE FIRM'S BUSINESS SOLUTIONS PRACTICE GROUP, AND HIS BROAD RANGE OF PROFESSIONAL AND CIVIC ACTIVITIES EXEMPLIFIES THE FIRM'S HERITAGE AND FUTURE.

IN ONE OF THE LARGEST PRO BONO PROGRAMS IN THE STATE, MEMBERS OF THE FIRM DEVOTE HUNDREDS OF HOURS EACH YEAR TO THE REPRESENTATION OF INDIGENTS THROUGH A SPECIAL PROGRAM DEVELOPED JOINTLY WITH COURTS OF HINDS COUNTY.

WITH DECADES OF VARIED EXPERIENCE IN THE PRACTICE OF LAW AND IN PUBLIC SERVICE, WILLIAM WINTER (LEFT) AND JOHN HAMPTON STENNIS PROVIDE SENIOR LEADERSHIP AND DIRECTION TO THE FIRM.

In 1908, two Jackson physicians, John Hunter and Harley Shands, purchased a modest frame house at the corner of North State and Manship streets, converting it into the capital city's first hospital. Soon after the facility opened its doors, the doctors realized the burdensome details of administration were interfering with their true calling: the practice of medicine. ✳ In late 1910, Hunter, a Presbyterian, and Shands, a Methodist, offered ownership of the eight-room, 14-bed hospital to their respective churches. When both denominations declined, the Mississippi Baptist Convention accepted the gift. On January 3, 1911, Mississippi Baptist Hospital was born. This modest facility was the predecessor of Mississippi Baptist Health Systems, Inc. (MBHS), the present-day parent company of Baptist Medical Center (BMC). It now encompasses a home health agency, clinics, and other organizations dedicated to meeting health care needs in 16 central Mississippi counties.

"More than a hospital, Baptist Health Systems was formed to create new programs, services, and partnerships that meet changing needs in the community and in the health care industry," explains Kurt Metzner, president and chief executive officer of Baptist Health Systems. "Our goal is to create the Jackson area's most comprehensive network of easily accessible, quality medical services."

Baptist Medical Center

BMC, the system's flagship facility, offers expertise in more than 25 medical specialties. The 560-bed hospital employs some 3,000 health care professionals, who collectively treat an average of 9,800 patients per month.

At a time when many hospitals have chosen to limit services to a handful of specialties, Baptist has gone the opposite route, offering a full spectrum of treatment programs and caring for patients throughout their entire life cycle. Historically, Baptist has seen more patients and introduced more new technologies than any other private hospital in Mississippi.

Once the setting for the first open-heart surgery performed in a private Mississippi hospital, Baptist remains a national leader in cardiology and cardiovascular surgery. In 1997, the Baptist Heart Center performed its 10,000th open-heart surgery. In addition to providing state-of-the-art care for cardiac patients, Baptist Heart Services serves as a referral resource for 25 partner hospitals in Mississippi through the Cardiac Emergency Network and the Mobile Cardiac Care Unit, which was the first of its kind in Mississippi.

The Cancer Center at Baptist treats more than 5,000 patients per year—the largest caseload among private hospitals in Mississippi. Through its Women's Services, Baptist provides preventive care, health screenings, and educational programs for women of all ages. Baptist's Comprehensive Breast Center, the only facility of its kind in the state, focuses on prevention, diagnosis, and treatment of cancer and other diseases of the breast.

The recently expanded Birthplace offers comprehensive care for maternity patients, including a neonatal intensive care unit, while the Sleep Disorders Center of Mississippi boasts the latest technology and expertise for treating insomnia and other sleep disorders. Baptist's Chemical Dependency Center was the first private, hospital-based drug and alcohol treatment center in Mississippi and is the foundation for Baptist Behavioral Health Services.

"The delivery and range of our services has broadened over the years, but our foundation of Christian-based, quality health care remains unchanged," says C. Gerald Cotton, MBHS executive vice president. "More than anything else, this tradition is what sets Baptist apart."

Once the setting for the first open-heart surgery performed in a private Mississippi hospital, Baptist Medical Center remains a national leader in cardiology and cardiovascular surgery. Dr. Charles O'Mara performs a heart procedure.

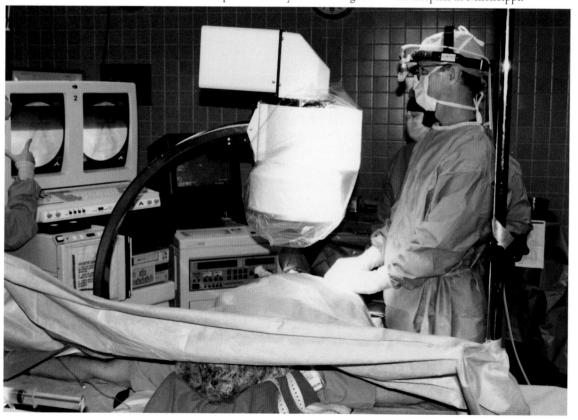

PREVENTIVE MEDICINE AND WELLNESS PROGRAMS

Baptist Health Systems is a leader in preventive health care. In 1996, Baptist teamed with Mississippi College to create the Baptist Healthplex at Mississippi College, a 106,000-square-foot family health and fitness center on the Mississippi College campus in Clinton. The Healthplex is jointly operated by Baptist, Mississippi College, and Healthcare Equities Group, Inc., a Michigan-based firm specializing in hospital-based fitness centers.

"The Baptist Healthplex is just one example of the great things that can result when organizations collaborate on health care delivery," Metzner says. "Forming partnerships like this one is a primary goal for Baptist Health Systems. Joint efforts like these result in significant health care improvements for the entire community."

Baptist Health Systems also operates the Baptist Fitness Center in downtown Jackson. Equipped with the latest in exercise equipment, an indoor swimming pool, and a walking track, the fitness center serves recovering patients as well as Jackson-area residents committed to improving their overall fitness.

Baptist takes preventive care into the community with health fairs and screenings in the workplace, at churches and community centers, and through educational programs in schools.

A FORWARD-THINKING SYSTEM

Baptist continues to invest in its downtown Jackson facilities. In 1998, the organization added a $25.6 million, 133,000-square-foot medical office building to the North State Street campus. Tenants include specialists in internal medicine, obstetrics and gynecology, cardiology, and dermatol-

ogy. In addition to providing much-needed space, the new building is a tangible symbol of Baptist's long-term commitment to the community.

Baptist Health Systems' future plans include development of a comprehensive geriatric program including assisted living facilities for senior citizens and expansion of the system's clinic network.

"In the years to come, we'll focus on being proactive and anticipating health care needs in the community," Metzner says. "Our long-term vision is to be the first choice of patients, physicians, and employees."

Hinds Community College

THE LARGEST OF MISSISSIPPI'S 15 COMMUNITY COLLEGE DISTRICTS IS SERVED BY Hinds Community College, which enrolls some 14,000 high school graduates and adult learners each year. Founded as an agricultural high school in 1917, Hinds began offering college-level courses in 1922. ✳ Today, more than 9,500 students register for the college's two-year degree programs, with another 4,500 signing up for workforce development and continuing education courses. Former

Mississippi Governor John Bell Williams, motivational speaker Zig Ziglar, businessman Warren Hood, State Supreme Court Justice Jim Smith, and country music star Faith Hill are all among Hinds' alumni.

The Hinds Community College district includes six locations serving five counties in west-central Mississippi. Sites include the Academic/Technical Center and Nursing/Allied Health Center, both located in Jackson; the Rankin, Raymond, and Utica campuses; and the Vicksburg-Warren County Branch. Students from Claiborne, Copiah, Hinds, Rankin, and Warren counties are all within 30 miles of a Hinds campus or branch.

AREAS OF SPECIALTY

Hinds offers more than 100 university transfer programs for academic students and more than 100 vocational-technical programs designed to prepare students for immediate entry into the workforce.

The college also has developed a number of specialized programs in response to the communities it serves. The Center for Emerging Technologies, for example, offers training programs designed specifically to meet the needs of Jackson's growing telecommunications industry.

The One-Stop Career Center provides career assessment, workforce readiness skills, and job placement, which matches qualified workers with suitable employers in the Jackson area; while the Institute for Creative Learning in Retirement offers classes for retirees, taught by retirees. Through

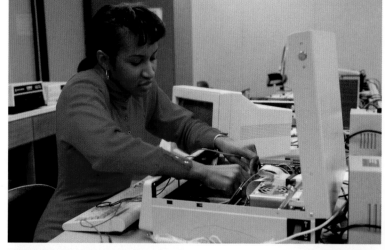

the International Trade Center, specialists in international trade provide free import and export counseling. Likewise, the Small Business Development Center offers management training, start-up assistance, market research, referrals, and other free services to local small-business owners.

Hinds is also a leader in workforce training. The college's $8 million Eagle Ridge Conference Center specializes in training for high-tech industries. Eagle Ridge is equipped with state-of-the-art technology, including video-conferencing, satellite uplinks and downlinks, and Internet access. The center is part of the Resource and Coordinating Unit for Economic Development, which has been recognized nationally for its innovative workforce training programs and has proved to be a valuable training resource for companies locating to or expanding in the Jackson area.

FLEXIBILITY

Hinds' academic and vocational programs are developed and scheduled according to student and community needs, helping to ensure that a quality education is available to anyone who wants it. Hinds offers courses addressing virtually every academic level, ranging from GED preparation to an academic honors program. Telecourses, evening and short courses, disability support services, computer-equipped learning assistance centers, job placement services, and child care facilities help students from all walks of life meet their educational goals.

Hinds awards more than $14 million in financial aid each year, including grants, loans, scholarships, and work-study programs. Approximately 70 percent of the college's students receive some form of financial assistance.

But Hinds does more than promise an affordable, quality education. Every degree comes with an iron-clad Student Guarantee. The college assures each student that credits earned at Hinds will transfer to the four-year college of his or her choice, or Hinds will provide up to nine additional credit hours tuition-free. In the voca-

tional-technical arena, Hinds guarantees that employers will be satisfied with graduates' skills, or the graduates may come back to Hinds for nine tuition-free credit hours of training in their field of study.

The college's 650 full- and part-time instructors enjoy a reputation for putting their students first. Honors won by individual instructors include three Professor of the Year awards from the Council for Advancement and Support of Education, the National Teacher of the Year Award from the Association of Community College Trustees, and the National Vocational Teacher of the Year Award.

Hinds' student-to-faculty ratio is 17-to-1, allowing personal instruction for every student. While academic instructors are required to hold master's degrees in their fields, a large percentage also hold doctoral degrees. Throughout the district, Hinds' vocational and technical instructors share expertise gained from years of solid, hands-on experience in their program areas, as well as holding advanced degrees in their fields.

EXTRACURRICULAR ACTIVITIES

Beyond academics, students can participate in more than 90 special-interest clubs and organizations active throughout the Hinds Community College district. Students enrolled at the Raymond and Utica locations may also choose to live on campus.

The college offers intramural athletics at two campuses, in addition to 10 varsity sports offered district-wide: men's football, baseball, golf, track, basketball, tennis, and soccer, as well as women's basketball, tennis, and softball.

Hinds is committed to helping athletes excel both on and away from the field. The college is a five-time recipient of the prestigious Halbrook Award, presented to Mississippi colleges and universities that consistently graduate a high percentage of athletes.

In spite of its tremendous growth over the years, Hinds continues to provide personal attention to every student and maintains its focus on serving the needs of the community. The college is banking on a bright future built on exceptional programs and services, all created to enhance the quality of life in the Jackson area.

A HINDS STUDENT READS *The American Short Story* AS PART OF HER ACADEMIC STUDIES. HINDS OFFERS MORE THAN 100 UNIVERSITY TRANSFER PROGRAMS, WHICH ARE ENTHUSIASTICALLY ACCEPTED BY SENIOR INSTITUTIONS THROUGHOUT THE STATE (LEFT).

HINDS COMMUNITY COLLEGE IS KNOWN THROUGHOUT THE STATE FOR ITS BEAUTIFUL BUILDINGS AND GROUNDS. THE STATE-OF-THE-ART CAFETERIA AND THE CLOCK/CARILLON TOWER ARE AMONG THE NEWEST ADDITIONS ON THE RAYMOND CAMPUS (RIGHT).

U.S. OFFICE PRODUCTS

U.S. OFFICE PRODUCTS (USOP) IS A SINGLE-SOURCE SUPPLIER FOR CORPORATE offices, providing office supplies, furniture, machines, printing, and office coffee services to companies throughout Mississippi. ✳ USOP's presence in the workplace can be as small as a paper clip or notebook, or as prominent as productivity-enhancing office furniture or custom-printed business forms. Mississippi's exclusive distributor of Starbucks® coffee,

USOP even handles that all-important morning java.

The Mississippi operating company was founded in Jackson in 1919 as The Office Supply Company. The firm changed its name to Business-Works following the 1995 acquisition by U.S. Office Products. Subsequently, in 1998, BusinessWorks adopted the U.S. Office Products name nationwide.

"While our roots are in the traditional office supply business, our affiliation with U.S. Office Products has broadened both our vision and our menu of products and services," says Jack Huguley, USOP Mississippi operating company president. "Companies can place one call to USOP to address a variety of needs."

U.S. OFFICE PRODUCTS
USOP is the fastest-growing, highest-net-profit company in the business products industry today.

It was founded in 1994 on a simple premise: bring together the world's best office products and business services entrepreneurs, and provide them with the resources to be a market leader. It was an idea whose time had come.

RICK HAWK

USOP experienced explosive growth, skyrocketing from $134 million in annualized revenue at its initial public offering in February 1995 to more than $3.5 billion by the end of 1997. Today, the company is one of the 100 largest firms traded on the Nasdaq exchange.

USOP has operations throughout the United States and in Canada, New Zealand, Australia, and the United Kingdom. The company's 19,000 employees annually deliver more than 40,000 office products, business services, and educational products to more than 1 million customers worldwide.

The USOP family of companies includes more than 185 successful businesses. Each company operates at a local level, with local management responsible and accountable for performance. The USOP network reduces procurement costs—

and headaches—by streamlining the number of suppliers within the network. The high-volume buying power, consolidated warehousing, centralized accounting, and inventory control available from USOP mean more products and services at more competitive prices. "By becoming a part of USOP, we increased our purchasing power tremendously, and went on to provide lower prices to our customers," Huguley says.

ONE-STOP SHOPPING

USOP also offers more convenient service for Mississippi customers, who include companies with anywhere from 50 to 1,000-plus employees. "Businesses today are looking for ways to simplify. They want to reduce the number of vendors they have to deal with every day, and streamline their purchasing processes. USOP fills that need with a broader spectrum of products and services than the competition," Huguley says. "It's one-stop shopping for our customers. Where else can they get office supplies, copiers and fax machines, office machine repair and maintenance, office furniture, printing, and even coffee and snacks, all from a single supplier? It's a powerful combination."

USOP is Mississippi's exclusive distributor for a number of upscale office furniture manufacturers, such as Herman Miller and Milcare health

systems furniture, and for office machine lines, including Ricoh and Panasonic, as well as the major supplier of Sharp, Canon, and Hewlett-Packard products. In addition to being the exclusive distributor of Starbucks premium coffee, USOP offers a unique brewing system that preserves coffee flavor and reduces waste.

USOP's fleet of trucks blankets the state, delivering products to desktops in virtually every city in Mississippi. In addition to the operating company headquarters in Jackson, USOP operates in Vicksburg, Greenville, Greenwood, Columbus, Tupelo,

Meridian, Laurel, and Hattiesburg. The company employs more than 275 Mississippians, including 50 technicians responsible for maintaining and servicing the company's office machines, computers, and other technology-oriented products.

"We're proud of how well we've made the transition from a local, independent distributor to a regional high-volume, low-cost provider," Huguley says. "USOP's combination of low prices and efficient operation has created a thriving, profitable distributorship that works for our customers, our employees, and our shareholders."

▲ RICK HAWK

U.S. OFFICE PRODUCTS HAS OPERATIONS THROUGHOUT THE UNITED STATES AND IN CANADA, NEW ZEALAND, AUSTRALIA, AND THE UNITED KINGDOM. THE COMPANY'S 19,000 EMPLOYEES ANNUALLY DELIVER MORE THAN 40,000 OFFICE PRODUCTS, BUSINESS SERVICES, AND EDUCATIONAL PRODUCTS TO MORE THAN 1 MILLION CUSTOMERS WORLDWIDE.

▲ RICK HAWK

ENTERGY CORPORATION AND ITS EMPLOYEES HAVE BEEN A PART OF THE GOOD life in Jackson for more than 75 years. The company name hasn't always been the same, but the core business of providing utility service and the core commitment to building Mississippi have been constant. ✳ Headquartered in New Orleans, the company began as a regulated monopoly, providing electricity and gas to a franchise area in the Mid-South region of the United States. Today,

Entergy has expanded to become a global competitor, owning and operating overseas power systems, and providing a diversified range of services.

LIGHTING THE WAY SINCE 1923

When entrepreneur Harvey Couch founded the handful of companies that would eventually become Entergy Corporation, electricity was still an oddity, largely limited to exhibits at the state fair. Only a small number of cities had their own power plants, and most of rural Mississippi still relied on kerosene lanterns. The state had even fewer paved roads than lightbulbs, and the very idea of bringing electricity to isolated communities seemed a far-fetched dream.

Electricity quickly moved from a technological marvel to a modern-day convenience. Today, separate Entergy business units provide power marketing services, sell electricity wholesale, and offer a broad range of energy management, security monitoring, and telecommunications services.

ENTERGY IN MISSISSIPPI

The familiar face of Entergy in Mississippi belongs to the people who maintain the lines and equipment that deliver electricity to nearly 400,000 homes and businesses in 45 of the state's 82 counties. And the familiar base of Entergy in Mississippi is the historic Electric Building in downtown Jackson.

From its very beginnings, Entergy made economic and community development one of its foremost missions. Realizing that the company would grow only as fast as the communities it served, Entergy's original leaders established an industrial development program during the company's first decade in business. Today, Entergy continues to work with local and state officials to attract new firms to Mississippi and create jobs for Mississippians.

Entergy's community development cornerstone is the highly successful Team City program. Launched in 1994, the program now includes more than two dozen Mississippi communities.

Entergy also provides financial support to many community and nonprofit organizations.

Entergy's nuclear operations are also based in Jackson. Echelon One serves as corporate headquarters for two nuclear subsidiaries. Entergy Operations manages Entergy's four domestic nuclear plants, and Entergy Nuclear, Inc. markets management services to other nuclear companies.

DIVERSIFICATION

The company's expansion into the security business reached Jackson in 1997, when Entergy Security bought the alarm monitoring division of Day Detectives. This acquisition made Entergy Security the largest provider of security systems in the Southeast and the sixth largest in the nation.

Entergy also introduced telecommunications services in 1997. Through a joint venture, Entergy-Hyperion Telecommunications offers competitive telephone services to commercial customers.

A CONTINUING COMMITMENT

As Mississippi moves toward a system that will allow consumers to choose their energy provider, Entergy is working to ensure that changes in the industry benefit the consumer. As the company moves into the next century, Entergy remains committed to the power of people—people who are Entergy team members and people who choose Entergy to provide power and other services. The ideals expressed by Couch in 1925 remain relevant: "The success of this system lies in our ability to change, and to explore new ways of doing things, all with the benefit to the customer as our goal."

THE HEADQUARTERS FOR ENTERGY'S NUCLEAR BUSINESSES IS ECHELON ONE IN NORTHWEST JACKSON (LEFT).

ENTERGY MAINTAINS THE LINES AND EQUIPMENT THAT DELIVER ELECTRICITY TO NEARLY 400,000 HOMES AND BUSINESSES IN 45 OF MISSISSIPPI'S 82 COUNTIES (RIGHT).

PAUL NEHRENZ

THE EDISON WALTHALL HOTEL

ACKSON IS HOME TO A NUMBER OF HOTELS, BUT FOR TRAVELERS IN SEARCH of elegant accommodations and exceptional guest services, the only choice is The Edison Walthall Hotel. Welcoming its first guests in 1928, the Walthall billed itself as a "superior quality hotel for coat-and-tie clientele." Since then, the handsome hotel in the heart of downtown has remained at the center of Jackson's business, political, and social life. Guests who check in at The Edison Walthall Hotel today enjoy luxurious accommodations and exceptional service in one of Jackson's most elegant landmarks.

ENHANCING AN ORIGINAL

Throughout its colorful history, the Walthall Hotel has changed ownership several times. In 1990, Edison Hotels and Resorts Company of Atlanta purchased the property, with plans to make the hotel a downtown focal point. Immediately, the company began a continuous renovation—not as a finite project, but as an ongoing process. Five percent of the hotel's revenues are allocated to upgrading what is already considered by many to be the finest hotel in the capital city. "We make enhancements every month," Earl Gaylor, president, says. "This hotel will only get better with age."

EXCEPTIONAL AMBIENCE AND AMENITIES

The luxury that awaits guests begins in the gracious lobby, where crystal chandeliers, exquisite woodwork, and original art establish an atmosphere of old-world elegance. "We make decorative selections that fit the styles popular at the time the hotel opened," Gaylor explains. "We've obtained a great deal of turn-of-the-century artwork and period-style fixtures in an effort to respect and preserve the hotel's heritage."

The luxury of the lobby overflows into each of the 208 spacious guest rooms and suites, where attention to detail is evident. The traditional decor includes new furniture and wall coverings, and each room has the modern convenience of computer jacks. Soft down pillows and top-of-the-line mattresses ensure a good night's rest.

The hotel also provides an elegant dining experience in its white-tablecloth restaurant, which combines palate-pleasing food and drink with a view of Capitol Street. The restaurant hosts a lavish Sunday brunch and a weekly champagne supper. Many guests gather in The Edison Walthall's cozy lounge nightly to enjoy evening cocktails and live piano music.

Guest amenities include a fitness center, heated swimming pool, in-room dining, free shuttle service to and from the airport and in the downtown area, guided tours of historic downtown Jackson, free indoor parking, valet service, a barbershop, and a gift shop and bookstore. With more than 7,000 square feet of meeting and banquet space, The Edison Walthall is also a popular site for dinner programs and wedding receptions.

Staffing at The Edison Walthall is equally outstanding. The hotel recruits and hires the top talent in the hospitality industry, and provides every employee—from concierge to bellhop—with extensive training.

THE PLACE TO STAY

With impeccable service and an atmosphere of intimate elegance, it's not surprising that The Edison Walthall has earned a reputation as the place to stay in Jackson. On a typical weekday, some 30 states and 50 cities are represented in The Edison Walthall register. The hotel also regularly is the choice of visiting celebrity performers, foreign diplomats, politicians, and titans of industry.

"There's a definite niche in Jackson for a superior hotel," Gaylor says. "We're committed not only to preserving the tradition of exceptional service and atmosphere originally established by the Walthall in 1928, but also to enhancing it over the years to come."

JACKSON IS HOME TO A NUMBER OF HOTELS, BUT FOR TRAVELERS IN SEARCH OF ELEGANT ACCOMMODATIONS AND EXCEPTIONAL GUEST SERVICES, THE ONLY CHOICE IS THE EDISON WALTHALL HOTEL (LEFT).

THE HOTEL ALSO PROVIDES AN ELEGANT DINING EXPERIENCE IN ITS WHITE-TABLECLOTH RESTAURANT, WHICH COMBINES PALATE-PLEASING FOOD AND DRINK WITH A VIEW OF CAPITOL STREET (RIGHT).

W HEN DEPOSIT GUARANTY NATIONAL BANK OPENED ITS DOORS FOR THE first time on June 15, 1925, a full-page ad in the *Jackson Clarion-Ledger* invited customers to "Come deposit, save, and grow with us." The bank's now-familiar motto Grow With Us is still as appropriate today as it was on that first day of business. ✳ Deposit Guaranty operates more than 200 banking locations in Mississippi, Louisiana, and Arkansas, including 31

full-service banks in Jackson. With total assets topping $6.8 billion and more than 3,500 employees systemwide, Deposit Guaranty is the largest bank holding company headquartered in Mississippi.

NEW OPTIONS IN BANKING

Deposit Guaranty has always been quick to provide its customers with the latest in banking products, services, and technology. It was the first bank in Mississippi to offer a bank

credit card, automated teller machines, loans by phone, electronic funds transfer services, and PC banking. Deposit Guaranty continues to lead the way in banking technology.

"Our customers have different preferences about how they want to access our products and services," says E.B. Robinson Jr., chairman of the board and CEO. "While the majority still value face-to-face relationships in traditional bank settings,

a growing number of customers want alternatives."

New products and services allow customers to interact with the bank on their own terms. Deposit Guaranty's remote banking products allow customers to conduct a number of financial transactions—including deposits, withdrawals, transfers, and bill payments—via telephone or computer. Deposit Guaranty's GNet Web site allows customers to request information and enroll in specific services without ever setting foot in a bank.

Electronic banking benefits both Deposit Guaranty and its customers. As more customers handle routine transactions electronically, frontline employees have more time to offer other more specialized services. Electronic banking also helps hold down operational costs for the bank. The cost of processing an electronic payment averages less than half the cost of processing a paper check.

"Our world is changing, and so are we," says Robinson. "That's one reason why so many people continue to come to us for financial services—even if they don't come to us in quite the same way as they did in the past."

Advanced services aren't limited to electronic banking. Several new products are card-based, created in response to customer demands for convenience. New card products include the Purchasing Card, which allows a business to pay for purchases with a card, then receive a consolidated statement; the Travel and Entertainment Card, similar to the Purchasing Card, but geared toward business travel and entertainment; and the Guaranty PayChek card, which allows companies who use direct deposit of payroll to include

WITH TOTAL ASSETS TOPPING $6.8 BILLION AND MORE THAN 3,500 EMPLOYEES SYSTEMWIDE, DEPOSIT GUARANTY NATIONAL BANK IS THE LARGEST BANK HOLDING COMPANY HEADQUARTERED IN MISSISSIPPI.

GIL FORD PHOTOGRAPHY

SCOT SLAY

employees who do not maintain checking accounts.

Even customers who still want face-to-face contact with a banker don't always have to make an extra trip to the bank. Many Deposit Guaranty customers do their banking at branches located in supermarkets or discount stores.

"In the past, convenience meant a drive-through window," Robinson says. "Now, it's a broader time management issue. Demands on people's time are extraordinary, and their patience with banks that don't respect that fact is nonexistent.

"These days, bringing business to the bank means bringing the bank to the customer," Robinson continues. "Our success depends on how far we're willing to go to earn and keep business. Today, as always, Deposit Guaranty is willing to go as far as it takes."

COMMUNITY INVOLVEMENT

Deposit Guaranty participates in a number of civic and charitable activities that not only generate a significant financial impact, but also enhance Mississippi's image and boost economic development efforts.

The Deposit Guaranty Golf Classic is one of 45 PGA TOUR events in the country and the only such event held in Mississippi. Held at Annandale Golf Club just north of Jackson, the tournament has an $8

million impact on the Jackson-area economy and focuses positive, national media attention on Jackson and Mississippi. The tournament proceeds are donated to local charities, including the Blair E. Batson Hospital for Children of the University of Mississippi Medical Center.

In 1996, the bank was a sponsor of the exclusive American appearance of the *Palaces of St. Petersburg: Russian Imperial Style.* This historic exhibit showcased Jackson as a cultural center and brought millions of tourism dollars into Mississippi. Deposit Guaranty's cultural support continued with the *Splendors of Versailles* exhibit in 1998.

In partnership with DREAM (Developing Resources for Education

in America), Deposit Guaranty supports an ongoing character education program in the elementary schools in its markets. The bank is also a primary sponsor of the Senior Olympics on both the district and statewide levels in Mississippi and Louisiana; a sponsor of the International Ballet Competition; and a strong supporter of Mississippi's artistic community. The Bank Marketing Association recognized Deposit Guaranty's outstanding civic efforts with the Gold Coin Award for community involvement.

"The idea of 'growing with us' applies not only to our customers, but to the city of Jackson and the other communities Deposit Guaranty serves," Robinson says. "What's good for Jackson is good for Deposit Guaranty."

CLOCKWISE FROM TOP LEFT: THE BANK IS A PRIMARY SPONSOR OF THE SENIOR OLYMPICS ON BOTH THE DISTRICT AND STATEWIDE LEVELS IN MISSISSIPPI AND LOUISIANA.

THE DEPOSIT GUARANTY GOLF CLASSIC IS ONE OF 45 PGA TOUR EVENTS IN THE COUNTRY AND THE ONLY SUCH EVENT HELD IN MISSISSIPPI. HELD AT ANNANDALE GOLF CLUB JUST NORTH OF JACKSON, THE TOURNAMENT HAS AN $8 MILLION IMPACT ON THE JACKSON-AREA ECONOMY.

DEPOSIT GUARANTY HAS ALWAYS BEEN QUICK TO PROVIDE ITS CUSTOMERS WITH THE LATEST IN BANKING PRODUCTS, SERVICES, AND TECHNOLOGY.

Stuart C. Irby Company and Irby Construction Company

The Stuart C. Irby Company and Irby Construction Company are power players in the electrical industry in Mississippi, across the United States, and around the world. One of the top 20 electrical distributors nationally, the Stuart C. Irby Company provides commercial and residential customers with the materials and know-how needed to meet their electrical requirements. ✳ The company was founded in Jackson in 1926 by Stuart C. Irby, an early advocate of electricity as an energy source for the rural South. Electrical construction projects dominated the company's early years, with Irby Construction Company organized as a separate operation in 1946. Irby Construction has built more than 150,000 miles of electrical lines in 42 states and in several foreign countries.

"These are companies focused on value," says Stuart M. Irby, president of Stuart C. Irby Company and grandson of the company's founder. "We offer the highest-quality products at the lowest possible cost, and provide superior service that adds an extra value beyond the product or service contract purchase price."

The Stuart C. Irby Company

The Stuart C. Irby Company operates 30 sales branches in Mississippi, Alabama, Arkansas, Florida, Louisiana, Oklahoma, Tennessee, and Texas. Eight of these branches are located in Mississippi, including an upscale lighting fixtures showroom in Ridgeland.

The company's customer list spans the industrial, utility, commercial, and residential markets. Stuart C. Irby Company supplies major industrial construction projects and manages the day-to-day electrical supply needs of manufacturers throughout the Southeast.

Investor-owned utilities, rural electric cooperatives, and municipal power systems throughout the South know they can depend on Stuart C. Irby Company for a quick response time, especially during emergencies. Irby supplies 418 electric utilities, which, in turn, service more than 12.5 million electric meters—a full 10 percent of all the meters in the United States.

Commercial customers include retail businesses, office buildings, and government facilities. Through its contractor customers, Stuart C. Irby Company supplies commercial construction projects of every size throughout the South. On the residential side, contractors, interior designers, architects, electricians, and individual home owners turn to Irby for the latest in electrical and lighting systems and upscale fixtures.

A Leader in Customer Service

Stuart C. Irby Company's pledge of superior service is backed by the industry's most knowledgeable experts and more than 70 years' experience in the electrical supply business. The company's 576 high-tech specialists, knowledgeable sales associates, and support staff bring 3,500 years of collective experience in the electrical products industry.

Another edge in the marketplace is Stuart C. Irby Company's close working relationship with its sister company, Irby Construction. "Our experience in construction gives Stuart C. Irby Company practical insight into the challenges faced by our contractor

IRBY CONSTRUCTION HAS BUILT MORE
THAN 150,000 MILES OF ELECTRICAL LINES
IN 42 STATES AND IN SEVERAL FOREIGN
COUNTRIES.

customers," Stuart M. Irby notes. "That kind of hands-on experience makes a real difference in the level of service we're able to offer."

IRBY CONSTRUCTION COMPANY

"We do not let obstacles stand in our way," says Charles Irby, president of Irby Construction Company. "Hand us a job, and this company finds a way to get it done."

The division of Stuart C. Irby Company that would eventually become Irby Construction built its first transmission line in 1917. Ever since that first 11-mile project, Irby Construction Company has been recognized as a pioneer in utility construction.

The company is a leader in every phase of power line and substation construction, maintenance, and emergency reconstruction, and is also a player in other fast-growth construction specialties, including fiber-optic ground wire systems and cellular communication towers.

Flexibility, financial stability, and turnkey experience make Irby Construction the company of choice for electrical construction projects of any size, anywhere. With the market for

its services expanding worldwide, Irby has completed projects in Africa, Southeast Asia, and Central America. A recent project included turnkey construction of the first transmission line ever built in the Central American country of Belize.

"We go where the work is, adapting to environments and circumstances to complete each project to the satisfaction of the customer," Charles Irby says. "We know our way around the world."

Irby continues: "Our difference is the quality of our work, the tight schedules we maintain, and our commitment to cost effectiveness. There is no job too tough for us to complete on time, within budget, and with good quality work."

AN EMPHASIS ON VALUES

Throughout their histories, Stuart C. Irby Company and Irby Construction have remained true to the business principles embraced by the companies' founder—principles based not only on traditional business practices and civil law, but also upon the Bible. The companies support a number of charitable causes, including Habitat for Humanity and United Way.

The Stuart C. Irby Company earmarks 10 percent of pretax profits for community support.

"We are companies interested in meeting the needs of others—our customers, our suppliers, our employees, and our community," Stuart Irby says. "We stress ethical business practices and respect for the individual. We want the Irby companies to be perceived not only as fiscally sound, but morally sound as well."

▶ J. L. STUDIOS

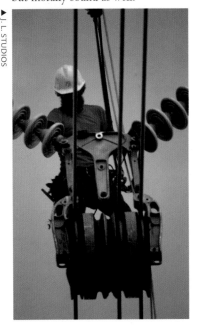

FLEXIBILITY, FINANCIAL STABILITY, AND
TURNKEY EXPERIENCE MAKE IRBY CON-
STRUCTION THE COMPANY OF CHOICE FOR
ELECTRICAL CONSTRUCTION PROJECTS OF
ANY SIZE, ANYWHERE.

M

ISSISSIPPI BUSINESSES HAVE RELIED ON THE COMPANY NOW KNOWN AS OffiSource to keep their offices furnished and their supply closets well stocked since 1928. Mississippi's oldest independent office products company, OffiSource provides office furniture, supplies, and printing to commercial and professional customers in Mississippi and Louisiana, and to those customers' branch offices in cities across the country.

The company's name has changed in the 70 years since the first supplies changed hands, but the OffiSource mission has always been the same—to remove obstacles and enhance other people's careers. "The products and services we sell make our customers' work more efficient, more effective, and more profitable," says Charles Hooker, president. "To the degree that

we help people acquire these necessities easily and less expensively, we're removing obstacles and enhancing their opportunities for success. That makes OffiSource more valuable to those we serve."

TAKING CARE OF BUSINESSES

OffiSource was created through the 1986 merger of two friendly business rivals—Mississippi Stationery Company, founded in 1928, and Standard Stationers, founded in 1938. Both companies were pioneers in the concept of contract office furnishings and supplies for larger firms, serving customers in Mississippi, Louisiana, and Arkansas, and were among the first office supply companies to offer interior design services. Building on that tradition, OffiSource continues to offer its customers more and better ways to get their jobs done.

OffiSource was one of the first firms to employ professional interior designers, who work hand in hand with architects and other design professionals to create functional, attractive office

atmospheres suited to each client's business needs and individual taste.

OffiSource is recognized as a leader in its field not only by virtue of its sales volume, but also by its exclusive representation of several upscale office furniture lines. OffiSource is the exclusive dealer for both Knoll, Inc. and Kimball Office Group, two of the world's leading office furniture manufacturers, and holds franchises with many of the other top names in office furniture.

The company's 35 employees stay up to speed on the latest products and technologies, and are able to make sound recommendations that save their customers time and money. "We're independently owned and independently minded, which ultimately benefits the customer," Hooker continues. "We're large enough to invest in the technologies, products, and people that keep us on the cutting edge, but we adapt quickly to changes in our customers' needs. We're a local company, we know our customers, and we never forget that *our* only job is to make *their* job easier."

OFFISOURCE PROVIDES OFFICE FURNITURE, SUPPLIES, AND PRINTING TO COMMERCIAL AND PROFESSIONAL CUSTOMERS IN MISSISSIPPI AND LOUISIANA, AND TO THOSE CUSTOMERS' BRANCH OFFICES IN CITIES ACROSS THE COUNTRY.

J.W. Underwood & Company

OUNDED IN 1948, J.W. UNDERWOOD & COMPANY HAS BEEN ONE OF Mississippi's most innovative real estate development firms. The company has developed some 27 communities and constructed more homes than any other Mississippi builder. The Underwood name is behind many of Jackson's most exclusive business and residential developments, with homes valued anywhere from $125,000 to more than $1 million. ✳ J.W. Underwood has been a pioneer in residential development for more than 50 years, introducing new construction and marketing concepts to the Mississippi real estate industry. Underwood was the first developer to focus on land-use planning and environmental design for both residential and commercial development, a concept the company continues to stress today.

New Areas of Residential Growth

J.W. Underwood & Company is credited with blazing new paths of residential growth for Jackson. The company is most famous for Crossgates, Mississippi's first large, master-planned community. The development of this 1,700-acre community included the construction of a 40-acre lake and the formation of a utility company to provide water and sewer service. Crossgates brought thousands of new residents to the east Jackson area, and made Brandon one of the metropolitan area's most prestigious addresses.

Blazing New Paths of Development

The Underwood Companies, a division of J.W. Underwood & Company, has taken an aggressive position of expansion to meet the challenging demands of the Metro Jackson marketplace, while maintaining solid developmental and construction practices. Underwood Homes, another division of J.W. Underwood & Company, built its reputation with a well-built three-bedroom, one-bath affordable home for everyone. It currently has expanded its residential offerings into larger single-residence homes, garden and patio homes, and upscale communities with sophisticated amenities that attract upper-end buyers.

Underwood Homes' first development on the reservoir, Windward

Oaks, completed in 1994, showed an active demand for these high-end homes. SUMMERS BAY on the Reservoir, Underwood Homes' current reservoir community, boasts a prestigious location next door to the Jackson Yacht Club. The waterfront and water-view residential lots and luxury patio homes, the security of a gated community, and the convenience of home owner boat slips has proved to be a great draw for Jackson-area home buyers.

Carlton Parke on Richardson Road, off Old Agency Road, in south Madison County features half-acre and larger lots in picturesque, rolling countryside with two small lakes. This exquisite, gated neighborhood offers a clubhouse, pool, and tennis court for its home owners. Activity looms large here also, with several families already in residence in stately homes and new construction evident.

Commercial Development

On the commercial side, J.W. Underwood & Company's Lakeover development is literally a city within a city. The largest office and business park in the Jackson metropolitan area, Lakeover stretches across the 1,250 wooded acres alongside Interstate 220 in north Jackson. Designed in harmony with the natural environment, Lakeover's centerpiece is an upscale office park overlooking two lakes. Long-term development plans call for the addition of hotels, banks, and service industries. Upon completion, the Lakeover development will be worth an estimated $250 million.

Renowned for its experience, innovation, integrity, and success in real estate development, J.W. Underwood & Company remains one of Mississippi's premier residential and commercial developers.

SUMMERS BAY on the Reservoir, Underwood Homes' current reservoir community, boasts a prestigious location next door to the Jackson Yacht Club.

The garden offices of J.W. Underwood & Company are located on Dogwood View Parkway in Lakeover.

WHEN ROBERT BARKSDALE OPENED AN INSURANCE AGENCY IN JACKSON IN 1933, he brought to the job a unique passion for both the business and its customers. The Robert Barksdale Company, Inc. soon earned a reputation as one of Mississippi's most forward-thinking insurance providers. When Barksdale died in the early 1960s, his widow, Mae Barksdale, was determined that a family member should continue to be a part of the

well-known company. Although she had never held a job outside the home, Mae Barksdale reported to work the next day at 7 a.m. and served the company for the next 25 years, finally retiring in 1987 at the age of 85. This same level of continuity and dedica-tion to serving the firm's clients has helped Barksdale Bonding & Insur-ance maintain its position as one of Mississippi's leading insurance agen-cies for more than 65 years. Today, the firm's guiding principles are still rooted in the founder's passion for service and meeting customer needs.

SPECIALISTS IN TRANSPORTATION, AVIATION, AND BENEFITS

While its clients are primarily located in Mississippi, Barksdale also serves businesses in Alabama, Georgia, Louisiana, Tennessee, Arkansas, and Texas. The company's diverse insur-ance expertise includes fleet trans-portation, agricultural and general aviation, construction, manufacturing, agriculture, and employee benefits and personal insurance.

Barksdale is Mississippi's largest insurer for commercial transportation, as well as agricultural and general avia-tion, and the state's largest group health provider. "One of Barksdale's strongest advantages is an expertise in niche markets that other insurance agencies can't match," says Charles Porter, Barksdale president. "Businesses that carry a high risk, like crop dust-ing or fleet trucking, need more than just a low premium. They need an insurer who understands the unique

risks involved in that business, and who has taken the time to research not only the insurance products out there, but also ways to minimize the risk in the first place."

Working with more than 25 under-writing firms, Barksdale provides pro-tection for contracting operations, trucking fleets, manufacturers, and large and small commercial accounts for property and casualty exposure, as well as group health.

The company is particularly

TONY STONE IMAGES, WALTER HODGES

TONY STONE IMAGES, ANDY SACKS

proactive in the transportation arena. In addition to maintaining relationships with established underwriters, Barksdale recruits qualified underwriting firms not currently handling fleet insurance and assists them in entering the business. The result is an expansive choice of underwriters that enables Barksdale to match its clients with uniquely qualified insurers at highly competitive rates. Barksdale established a sales office in Nashville specifically to serve the Southeast's growing transportation market.

Barksdale has long been an industry leader in employee benefits. While that has traditionally meant the establishment of pension and profit-sharing plans, today the focus is on health care. With health care plans, laws, and regulations changing daily, Barksdale's benefits specialists focus not only on keeping abreast of industry developments, but also on creating new plans that help the company's clients offer attractive benefits at affordable rates. A growing list of clients in the benefits arena prompted Barksdale to establish a satellite group health and life insurance sales office in Mobile.

The firm's depth of experience in every aspect of risk management enables Barksdale to adapt successful programs developed for one industry and apply them to others. This approach has led Barksdale to innovative methods of problem solving that benefit clients in every field.

Mississippi's Only Loss Control Department

Barksdale Bonding & Insurance is the only Mississippi insurance agency with an in-house Loss Control Department. The company's loss control experts develop risk management programs that actually reduce the likelihood of a catastrophe. This focus on loss control not only makes day-to-day operations safer, but often lowers a client's insurance premiums from day one. The Loss Control Department researches each client's industry to determine whether certain precautions or procedures exist that may qualify the client for preferential rates. The Loss Control Department then audits the client's

individual operations and makes recommendations that may lower premiums.

Barksdale has always viewed loss prevention to be equally as important as loss coverage. A number of Mississippi businesses claim to owe their survival to Barksdale's emphasis on loss control. For example, many of Barksdale's clients balked at the notion that they needed flood insurance. Those companies that took the agency's advice and purchased the extra coverage were among those still in business following the devastating Easter flood of 1979—a disaster that shut down dozens of Jackson companies for good.

"Beginning with a small company and helping it survive, grow, and thrive is the most rewarding aspect of our job," Porter says. "We're not

only protecting our clients' businesses today, we're protecting their potential for tomorrow."

Barksdale Bonding & Insurance has undergone three ownership changes since its founding in 1933, but the company's business philosophy is still based on principles established by Robert Barksdale. "Our employees are young, energetic, and creative, and our insurance programs are cutting edge. We combine those ingredients with exceptional service that's been a tradition ever since Robert Barksdale opened this firm," says Porter, who has been with the company since 1976. "Five, 10, 20 years from now and beyond, we still want to be known as the firm that offers not only top-notch, proactive service, but offers it continuously and reliably."

BARKSDALE HAS ALWAYS VIEWED LOSS PREVENTION TO BE EQUALLY AS IMPORTANT AS LOSS COVERAGE.

THE LEVEL OF CONTINUITY AND DEDICATION IN SERVING THE FIRM'S CLIENTS HAS HELPED BARKSDALE BONDING & INSURANCE TO MAINTAIN ITS POSITION AS ONE OF MISSISSIPPI'S LEADING INSURANCE AGENCIES FOR MORE THAN 65 YEARS.

CANIZARO TRIGIANI ARCHITECTS

ACKSON'S ECONOMY AND CULTURE HAVE PROVIDED OPPORTUNITIES FOR CANIZARO Trigiani Architects for more than half a century. Working with visionary clients, the firm has enriched the environment with projects as varied as the elegant Millsaps Buie House, the technically sophisticated Jackson International Airport, and the healing atrium at the Mississippi Methodist Rehabilitation Center. ✳ Canizaro Trigiani Architects (CTA) is one of the largest architectural,

THIS PAGE, CLOCKWISE FROM TOP LEFT: JACKSON INTERNATIONAL AIRPORT, ST. DOMINIC GARAGE, AND ECCO ITALIAN DESIGNS

OPPOSITE, CLOCKWISE FROM TOP LEFT: MILLSAPS-BUIE HOUSE, GRAND GULF VISITORS' CENTER, MISSISSIPPI METHODIST REHABILITATION CENTER PATIENT ROOM, ST. FRANCIS CATHOLIC CHURCH, MISSISSIPPI METHODIST REHABILITATION CENTER ATRIUM, AND JACKSON STATE UNIVERSITY DORM

planning, and interior design firms in Mississippi, and has developed a regional practice based on technical, corporate, health care, religious, institutional, and residential projects. The firm's creative solutions have consistently won recognition from professional organizations, including more than 25 local and regional design awards. Most important, CTA has earned the loyalty of its clients. More than 80 percent of the firm's work is for repeat clients, such as the University of Mississippi Medical Center and Trustmark

National Bank. "Our success rests on two principles," David Trigiani says. "First, our staff is committed to giving undivided attention for whatever time is necessary to meet our clients' needs. Additionally, our clients understand that good design can benefit the entire community."

Founded by James T. Canizaro in 1938, the firm earned a reputation for innovation, with work that included the Science Center at the University of Mississippi, St. Michael's Catholic Church in Biloxi, and the St. Dominic Hospital in Jackson. Today, the firm's leaders—Robert Canizaro, FAIA; David Trigiani, FAIA; Danny Cawthon, AIA; Steve Davis, AIA; and Kevin Lovell, AIA—are building on that legacy of innovation. "We never approach a project with a predetermined idea of the end result," Robert Canizaro says. "Each solution is a collaboration with the client. That relationship is the single most important source for the inspiration that ultimately defines the project."

Involved clients are only one reason for CTA's success. To ensure quality, the entire staff aims for effective communication and technical

expertise. "The public believes we only decide how buildings look," says Davis, "but in reality, we must learn the needs of the client first. We must enter the client's world, and discover the most efficient way to meet their needs." CTA's design process combines creativity and economy to resolve issues such as function, image, energy, safety, and maintenance. Ten registered architects and three certified interior designers provide the experience to address the complexities of today's architecture. The latest computer technology is incorporated into every aspect of the firm's activities. Professional services include master planning, programming, building and interior design, and facilities management.

Canizaro Trigiani Architects is also looking to the future. The firm's services—which have changed over the past 60 years—continue to evolve. Through regularly studying new design, management, and construction technologies, the firm is better able to serve the client. Cawthon says, "We are working hard to improve tomorrow's environment and create buildings of which we and our clients can be proud."

PERRY RICHARDSON

HAROLD HEAD

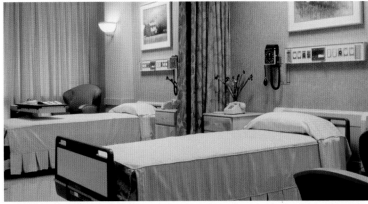

THE GOOD LIFE

BRUNINI, GRANTHAM, GROWER & HEWES, PLLC

NE OF MISSISSIPPI'S OLDEST AND LARGEST LAW FIRMS, BRUNINI, GRANTHAM, GROWER & Hewes, PLLC traces its beginnings to John B. Brunini, who began his practice in Vicksburg, Mississippi, in the latter part of the 19th century. The son of Italian immigrants who sought opportunity as farmers in America, Brunini was a testimony to the rewards that America granted to individual industry and integrity. Self-educated in the legal field, Brunini began practicing in 1891. He quickly established a solid reputation not only in Vicksburg, but also throughout Mississippi, achieving prominence in statewide business and legal affairs.

Brunini was joined in the practice by his two sons: Alexander, who came aboard in 1929, and Edmund, who joined in 1934. In 1946, John Brunini presided over the creation of the firm's Jackson office, which was eventually headed by his son Edmund.

Originally established to serve the legal needs of the booming oil and gas industry, the Jackson office eventually separated from its Vicksburg parent, quickly becoming one of Mississippi's most respected general practice firms.

"MANY OF OUR FIRM MEMBERS HAVE A DISTINGUISHED HISTORY OF SERVICE AND LEADERSHIP IN OUR STATE AND LOCAL BAR ASSOCIATIONS," SAYS ED BRUNINI JR. "THESE LAWYERS HAVE MATCHED OR SURPASSED THE ACHIEVEMENTS OF THE FOUNDING BRUNINI MEMBERS."

EXPERTISE IN COMMERCIAL, LITIGATION, AND REGULATORY LAW

Today, the Brunini, Grantham, Grower & Hewes team includes some 50 attorneys and 18 paralegals, offering considerable expertise in virtually every major practice field. The firm's clients consist primarily of business corporations, including a number of Fortune

500 companies. Brunini, Grantham, Grower & Hewes offers the complete range of services that a corporate client in Mississippi might need.

Attorneys in the commercial department offer expertise in general corporate law, real estate, securities, mergers and acquisitions, banking, insurance regulation, estate planning, syndications, and corporate and personal tax law.

Two litigation sections handle a wide range of cases involving complex commercial construction, employment, environmental, product liability, medical malpractice, contract, mass tort, bankruptcy, antitrust, securities, and tax issues in federal and state courts.

The regulatory practice includes legislative advocacy, environmental regulation, natural resources development and regulation, health care, and public utilities. Brunini, Grantham, Grower & Hewes' environmental practice group is acknowledged as a statewide leader in the rapidly growing field of environmental law.

The firm also practices extensively before the Mississippi Public Service Commission, representing gas, water, and sewer companies, as well as telecommunications clients.

BUSINESS, CIVIC, AND PROFESSIONAL LEADERSHIP

"Many of our firm members have a distinguished history of service and leadership in our state and local bar associations," says Ed Brunini Jr., grandson of the firm's founder and the third generation of the Brunini family to serve as a partner in the practice. "These lawyers have matched or surpassed the achievements of the founding Brunini members. If they were alive today, the firm's founders would be justifiably proud of the accomplishments of those who followed their lead."

The firm's attorneys have served as leaders in many organizations key to enhancing the quality of life in the

capital city. Individual attorneys have served as chairman or president of the United Way, Ballet Mississippi, Mississippi Museum of Art, New Stage Theatre, Young Jacksonians for the Symphony, Jackson Boys' Club, and Capital City Kiwanis Club.

The firm's lawyers also hold leadership positions within the Metro Jackson Chamber of Commerce and Mississippi ETV, as well as in numerous social and recreational clubs, schools, and churches.

In the professional arena, Brunini, Grantham, Grower & Hewes attorneys have served in positions such as chairperson of the Young Lawyers Division of the American Bar Association, assembly speaker of the Young Lawyers Division of the American Bar Association, president of the Mississippi State Bar

Young Lawyers Division, president of the Jackson Young Lawyers Section, and chairperson of the Mississippi Law Institute. Members of the firm have also served as president of the Natural Resources, Real Estate, Public Law, Wills and Estates, and Health Law sections of the Mississippi Bar Association.

"We believe the firm owes its current status as a highly successful business to the vibrancy of Jackson and the Jackson metropolitan area," says George P. Hewes III, senior member of the firm. "Our lawyers and staff believe passionately in Jackson's business and cultural future. We demand of each other sacrifice and commitment in meeting our duty of service to this community, and we believe that we'll play a prominent role in shaping its destiny."

THE BRUNINI, GRANTHAM, GROWER & HEWES MANAGEMENT TEAM INCLUDES (SEATED, FROM LEFT) ROBERT D. DRINKWATER, R. DAVID KAUFMAN, RICHARD W. DORTCH, (STANDING, FROM LEFT) CHRISTOPHER A. SHAPLEY, ED BRUNINI JR., AND BROOKS EASON.

St. Dominic Health Services, Inc.

In the early 1940s, a group of Jackson businessmen contacted the Dominican Sisters of Springfield, Illinois, with a business offer that would change the face of health care in the capital city. With their excellent reputation for compassionate care, the Springfield Dominicans were asked by these businessmen to assume operation of the 75-bed Jackson Infirmary. In April 1946, seven of the sisters arrived in Jackson to assume their new ministry. ✳ Almost immediately, the sisters announced plans to expand. In 1949, they purchased 20 acres on Lakeland Drive—then considered far outside the city proper—as the site for a large, modern hospital. In 1954, their dream was realized with the dedication of St. Dominic Hospital.

St. Dominic has expanded many times since its founding, adding hundreds of thousands of square feet in facilities and introducing many centers of excellence to the Jackson community. To better meet the challenges of the future, St. Dominic Health Services, a holding company with a number of newly organized subsidiaries, was created in 1985. St. Dominic-Jackson Memorial Hospital then became, and still is, the largest subsidiary in the total corporation. Today, the complex towers over Lakeland Drive, covering 42 acres, housing 571 beds, and employing more than 1,700 physicians, nurses, and skilled technicians.

Throughout its growth, St. Dominic has remained true to the original mission of the seven founding sisters: caring for all people with respect for their personal worth and dignity.

"St. Dominic was founded and is still operated by people who believe that all human life is sacred," says Sister Mary Dorothea Sondgeroth, president of St. Dominic Health Services, Inc. "St. Dominic combines a physical and a spiritual approach for a full circle of care. We offer sophisticated technology, administered lovingly and with compassion.

"People find this to be not just a curing place, but a healing place," continues Sondgeroth. "And healing the soul can often compensate for physical pain and loss."

◀ Medical Specialties

Since performing its first open-heart surgery in 1974, St. Dominic has been recognized as an outstanding cardiac care facility. According to the Mississippi Department of Health, the hospital's Mississippi Heart Institute (MHI) leads the state in the number of cardiac procedures performed, logging more than 3,500 open-heart surgeries and treatment procedures each year.

The MHI is the only cardiac care facility in Mississippi that has been invited to join the prestigious National Cardiovascular Network. Made up of 40 cardiovascular centers nationwide, the network chooses its members based not only on the quantity of procedures performed, but also on their outcomes.

St. Dominic's Hand Management Center, the only facility in Mississippi dedicated to physical and occupational therapy for the upper body extremities, offers job site evaluation, treatment of chronic pain, arthritis care, wound care, and pre- and postoperative care—all with an eye toward restoring function and helping patients return to work. For many people, loss or impairment of using their hands, arms, wrists, or shoulders can mean loss of livelihood.

Other innovative programs launched by St. Dominic include the $6 million Cancer Center, the most comprehensive radiation oncology facility in Mississippi; the state's first Lithotripsy Center, which uses shock wave therapy as a noninvasive, relatively painless method of eliminating kidney stones; and HealthLine/St. Dominic's, a community wellness program that offers free lectures, health screenings, and fitness tests.

Off-Site Facilities

St. Dominic Health Services owns and operates St. Catherine's Retirement

In April 1946, seven Dominican Sisters from Springfield, Illinois, arrived in Jackson at the request of a group of Jackson businessmen to assume the operation of the Jackson Infirmary, which later became St. Dominic Health Services.

Covering 42 acres at the intersection of Lakeland Drive and Interstate 55 in Jackson, St. Dominic employs more than 1,700 people dedicated to the Christian mission of healing begun by the Dominican Sisters in 1946.

KAY HOLLOWAY PHOTOGRAPHY

Village, Mississippi's only life care retirement community. St. Catherine's offers independent living, assisted living, and skilled nursing care in a beautifully designed setting. Located in nearby Madison, just north of Jackson, St. Catherine's Village is home to residents from 10 states.

Campbell Cove, a residential Alzheimer's facility located adjacent to St. Catherine's, allows patients suffering from Alzheimer's disease to function at their highest possible levels in a secure environment.

CHARITABLE AND COMMUNITY INVOLVEMENT

In addition to its high standards of health care excellence, St. Dominic Health Services supports more than 60 nonprofit, community, and performing arts organizations, donating time and resources to everything from Habitat for Humanity to the Mississippi Symphony Orchestra, and from Adopt-A-School to the Red Beans and Rice Festival, which benefits the Stewpot Community Services.

St. Dominic has won a number of awards for both its health care efforts and its service to the community. For example, the American Cancer Society has recognized the hospital's outstanding education and treatment programs. Both St. Dominic and St. Catherine's Village have been named Outstanding Business of the Year by the MetroJackson Chamber of Commerce. When Mississippi's first lady, Pat Fordice, launched a

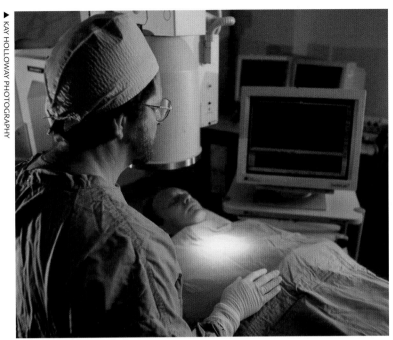

statewide cardiac screening and education campaign in 1997, she called upon St. Dominic to develop the prototype program.

In keeping with its mission to care for all persons, two community outreach ministries were begun by St. Dominic Health Services to provide medical attention to the underserved population in the Jackson area. The Care-A-Van—a 42-foot, mobile screening unit—conducts health screenings year-round at senior centers, Boys and Girls Clubs, and area public and parochial schools. And in 1996, St. Dominic joined forces with the Central Urban Ministry Center to open the Community Health Clinic to serve people of the inner city whose medi-cal needs were not being met by mainstream health care.

PREVENTION: THE KEY TO A HEALTHIER FUTURE

For St. Dominic, the key to the future of health care is prevention. As such, the organization has focused on developing programs that lead to permanent lifestyle improvements. "Most hospital stays today are not a result of disease, but of lifestyle," Sondgeroth explains. "Our ministry emphasizes respecting individuals. Part of that ministry lies in challenging people to respect themselves, and giving them the information they need to take charge and assume responsibility for their own health."

St. Dominic Health Services' agenda for the next century includes programs that help individuals with maintaining a healthy weight, coping with stress, and succeeding with smoking cessation. Free health screenings and educational programs in local schools, the community, and the workplace raise awareness of steps people can take to improve their own health.

"By creating programs that promote healthier lifestyles, we're taking a proactive role in shaping a healthier community," Sondgeroth says. "And not only will people feel better, but they'll actually help reduce their own health care costs."

MISSISSIPPI HEART INSTITUTE physicians have blended teamwork, technology, and tradition to develop a reputation of cardiac care excellence in the state of Mississippi.

HEALTHLINE, ST. DOMINIC'S CORPORATE and community wellness program, offers wellness lectures, health screenings, and fitness tests—all with an emphasis on helping individuals develop healthy lifestyles.

BLUE CROSS & BLUE SHIELD OF MISSISSIPPI

IN THE EVER CHANGING WORLD OF HEALTH CARE, IT'S LITTLE WONDER SO MANY individuals and firms put their trust in Blue Cross & Blue Shield of Mississippi. The company's reputation for rock-solid reliability is built on a half-century of service to its neighbors. Today, Blue Cross & Blue Shield of Mississippi is the largest health insurer in the state and boasts the state's most comprehensive network of providers. ✳ The company's history reveals more humble beginnings. Blue Cross & Blue

Shield of Mississippi got its start in October 1947, when eight community leaders signed a $10,000 promissory note to charter a Blue Cross plan in Mississippi. The company's first "office" was a borrowed corner; early employees had to wonder if the idea of a prepaid health care plan would catch on. But it did, and by 1949, the plan boasted more than 30,000 members.

Blue Cross & Blue Shield now serves some 915,000 Mississippians, including beneficiaries of Medicare. The company also serves Medicare beneficiaries in Louisiana, Missouri, and 12 other states. Blue Cross and Blue Shield processes an average of 7 million claims per year, which represent more than $3.5 billion paid in customer benefits.

Blue Cross & Blue Shield of Mississippi has grown to encompass several subsidiary and affiliated companies, including Advanced Health Systems, Inc.; Bluebonnet Life Insurance Company; Mississippi Insurance Marketing Agency; Employer Benefits Administrators, Inc.; and HMO of Mississippi, Inc.

SETTING THE STANDARD

One of 56 independent licensees of the national Blue Cross and Blue Shield Association, Blue Cross & Blue Shield of Mississippi consistently ranks among the system's top 10 performers. From electronic submission of claims to the creation of cost-saving managed care strategies, Blue Cross and Blue Shield leads the way in introducing insurance innovations to the state.

In 1988, the company initiated one of its most effective cost-containment programs ever, the Key Physician Network. This program provides customers with a choice of physicians throughout the state who accept the Blue Cross and Blue Shield allowable charge for their services. Further savings came in the early 1990s with the Community Pharmacy Network, which allows Mississippi pharmacies to offer reduced prices to Blue Cross and Blue Shield subscribers.

In the mid-1990s, the company added other strategies to curb rising costs, including preadmission certification and utilization and case management. The company also became a leader in the development of family-friendly work policies. Company Kids, an on-site child care facility, opened in 1994.

As the year 2000 approaches, the company is customizing its network offerings and benefit designs to meet the specific needs of customers. Through a strengthened relationship with the medical community, the company has developed programs designed to manage costs while ensuring quality of care.

Other advances include the expansion of the company's data capabilities, making its vast storehouse of electronic information one of its greatest strengths. In addition, Blue Cross and Blue Shield has created health and wellness programs, and enhanced existing training programs that ensure employees are kept abreast of changes associated with managed care.

A DEDICATED WORKFORCE

To meet its mission to "exceed the expectations of customers and providers," Blue Cross & Blue Shield of Mississippi relies on a dedicated workforce of more than 900 people. The

EMPLOYEES WORK AROUND THE CLOCK AT THE COMPANY'S OFFICES ON LAKELAND DRIVE, ENSURING CUSTOMERS ARE PROVIDED WITH EXCELLENT SERVICES.

majority of its employees work in the company's Jackson headquarters, while others are stationed in regional offices in Biloxi, Columbus, Hattiesburg, Southaven, and Tupelo, Mississippi.

The hardworking staff has earned the company many accolades, including the prestigious Brand Excellence Award, presented by the Blue Cross and Blue Shield Association. The Mississippi company received the award in 1996 and 1997 in recognition of its achievements in customer service, loyalty, brand strength, marketing, and financial performance.

COMMITMENT TO THE COMMUNITY

The commitment of Blue Cross and Blue Shield employees stretches to encompass the Jackson community. The company, for example, produces and helps staff Kid Zone, an annual two-day family festival and fund-raiser for children's charities. Employees also hit the pavement every year during the March of Dimes WalkAmerica. Blue Cross and Blue Shield has twice been the top annual corporate fund-raiser for the Mississippi March of Dimes.

In addition, employees lend a helping hand through a volunteer force known as the Blue Crew. In a typical year, the group provides more than 3,500 hours of community service for various nonprofit organizations.

Company employees have also gone the extra mile in times of emergency. When the Easter flood of 1979 sent the Pearl River flowing into company headquarters, the staff waded into waist-deep water to recover all-important customer files. They did everything possible to process claims promptly, and even salvaged paperwork by using irons and hair dryers.

REACHING OUT, REACHING FORWARD

Blue Cross & Blue Shield of Mississippi is dedicated to making a difference in the community. In 1992, the company established the nonprofit Mississippi Child Caring Foundation, which provides primary and preventive health care benefits to children who cannot afford private insurance and who are not eligible for government aid.

The company also sponsors the Design for Good Health art contest, a scholarship competition for students, and the Stuffee Program, which reaches some 20,000 youngsters each year with messages about healthy lifestyles.

Blue Cross & Blue Shield of Mississippi is committed to continuing its long-standing tradition of service to its neighbors. Now, as in 1947, the company's mission remains rock solid: to make sure Mississippians have access to the best and most affordable health care possible.

HELPING PROVIDE QUALITY HEALTH CARE TO ALMOST 1 MILLION MISSISSIPPIANS IS A MAJOR AND COMPLEX RESPONSIBILITY. BUT THE EMPLOYEES OF BLUE CROSS & BLUE SHIELD OF MISSISSIPPI ALWAYS KEEP THEIR FOCUS ON THE INDIVIDUALS THEY ARE SERVING.

WLBT-TV

WLBT SIGNED ON THE AIR ON DECEMBER 28, 1953. IN THE DECADES SINCE that first broadcast, the NBC affiliate has become Mississippi's most watched television station, earning a reputation for hard-hitting news coverage and strong editorial stands. More Mississippians turn to WLBT for news, weather, sports information, and entertainment than to any other media source in the state. More than just Mississippi's most reliable source for news and entertainment, WLBT acts as an advocate for those in need and a catalyst for positive change in the communities it serves.

AWARD-WINNING NEWS COVERAGE

WLBT has never hesitated to report on a story or issue impacting the people of Mississippi. The station has taken many controversial editorial stands and conducted investigations that have exposed corruption, warned consumers about scams, and put government officials and politicians on notice that they will be held accountable.

The station produces 37 half-hour newscasts per week, as well as constant updates of the latest-breaking news and weather developments. The WLBT news team is recognized as the best in the state and enjoys a national reputation for excellence.

WLBT has earned hundreds of honors and is the only television station in Jackson to have won a Peabody Award, the most prestigious national news award in television. The station has also won Emmy and Iris awards, which are presented nationally for outstanding news coverage. In addition, WLBT has received numerous honors from the Associated Press and the Mississippi Association of Broadcasters.

CLOCKWISE FROM TOP LEFT:
WITH MORE THAN 50 YEARS OF BROAD-CAST SERVICE, WOODIE ASSAF MAY WELL BE ONE OF WLBT'S MOST BELOVED AN-CHORS. GENERATIONS HAVE TURNED TO WOODIE IN EVERY WEATHER EMERGENCY.

A MEMBER OF THE 6 P.M. ANCHOR TEAM, MARSHA THOMPSON DELIVERS BREAKING NEWS AND LEGISLATIVE COVERAGE.

MORE MISSISSIPPIANS WATCH WLBT THAN ANY OTHER NEWS SOURCE. THE AWARD-WINNING WLBT 10 P.M. TEAM CONSISTS OF ROB JAY, MAGGIE WADE, HOWARD BALLOU, AND WALT GRAYSON.

PUBLIC SERVICE

WLBT is legendary for its public service efforts, using its unique position as Mississippi's most watched television station to spread the word about people in need. The station's IN TOUCH program has staff members of WLBT-TV meet with community groups and organizations to listen to their concerns. News stories developed from IN TOUCH meetings help solve problems in those communities. Millions of dollars have been raised by WLBT-TV for tornado, hurricane, and flood victims in their time of need. Telethons for charitable organizations such as Easter Seals and the United Negro College Fund have also raised millions of dollars for student scholarships and those with special physical needs. Through the regularly scheduled news segment "Wednesday's Child," which features children in need of adoptive families, more than 400 children have found homes. The annual Santa's Toy Chest promotion has collected more than 75,000 toys for the Toys for Tots program. WLBT's regular *Crimestoppers* show, which features reenactments of actual crimes, has brought hundreds of

criminals to justice. WLBT-TV has contributed to the communities it serves in so many ways, its role is more of a trusted friend than a television station.

THE LATEST TECHNOLOGY

WLBT has invested millions of dollars to ensure that its viewers receive the best possible service. With its 2,000-foot tower and Channel 3 frequency, WLBT's audience reach and picture quality are unmatched by any other television station in Mississippi. The station's transmitter and studio facilities are state-of-the-art. WLBT

also operates Mississippi's first and only television news helicopter; SKYCOPTER 3 provides fast coverage of news events taking place in hard-to-access areas and live broadcasts from the skies above Jackson. The station's greatest resource is its talented staff, which boasts an average tenure of 15 years with WLBT.

Assuming a leadership role not only in reporting the news and providing entertainment, but also in making the state a better place to live, WLBT-TV touches the lives of Mississippians every day.

IN THE EARLY DAYS OF TELEVISION, ANCHORS WORE MANY HATS. THE WEATHER ANCHOR MIGHT ALSO DO LIVE COMMERCIALS OR SPORTS REPORTS, AND WOODIE DID JUST THAT.

WITH SKYCOPTER 3, WLBT NEWS TAKES VIEWERS TO NEW HEIGHTS, SHOWING THEM ACTION FIRSTHAND. WLBT ANCHOR BERT CASE AND PILOT COYT BAILEY PREPARE FOR TAKEOFF.

VICKERS, INCORPORATED

WHEN IT COMES TO POWER AND MOTION CONTROL TECHNOLOGY, THE Vickers Fluid Power Division's products, experience, and expertise are industry pacesetters. The world leader in advanced technology fluid power, Vickers manufactures products for aerospace, marine, and defense markets worldwide. ✳ The company understands every aspect of the fluid power and fuel pump products business because it helped define the industry.

Since 1921, Vickers, Incorporated has led the way in developing new technologies and manufacturing processes, as well as providing the industry's most comprehensive customer service.

The Fluid Power Division of Vickers, Incorporated operates state-of-the-art manufacturing and product support facilities in the United States, Europe, and the Far East. A 270,000-square-foot facility in Jackson serves as the division's world headquarters.

A LEGACY OF INNOVATION

In 1921, a young machinist named Harry Vickers founded the Vickers Manufacturing Company in Los Angeles. Specializing in the design and production of hydraulic machinery, the new company had no assets and was staffed by a single part-time employee.

But under Harry Vickers' capable leadership, the fledgling company played a starring role in shaping the fluid power industry. By 1937, Vickers, Incorporated was a leading manufacturer of the hydraulic pumps, valves, and controls used in aircraft, machine tool, construction, and mining applications.

The spirit of innovation that originally led Vickers to international prominence continues today. The founder's fledgling company has grown to include more than 9,000 employees serving customers worldwide. Vickers products include hydraulic pumps, motors, and cylinders; electronic and hydraulic controls; electric motors and drives; filters; and fluid evaluation products and services.

Today, Vickers, Incorporated is composed of three groups: the Industrial Group, the Electronic Systems Group, and the Aerospace Marine Defense Group, which includes the Vickers Fluid Power Division.

VICKERS PRODUCTS AND APPLICATIONS

The Fluid Power Division produces and services some 400 products and more than 30,000 components worldwide, from a tiny torpedo actuator that fits in the palm of one's hand, to a 300-gallon-per-minute gear pump used to steer U.S. Navy destroyers. Vickers products and systems are found in top-of-the-line commercial, commuter, and military aircraft, on board ships and submarines, and in tanks and combat vehicles around the world.

Today, Vickers is the world's leading supplier of hydraulic components for commercial aviation. The majority of wide-body jets in flight use Vickers engine-driven pumps to generate primary hydraulic power. In fact, at least one Vickers component is found aboard every major commercial aircraft built in the world today.

THE STRINGENT QUALITY AND RELIABILITY STANDARDS OF THE AEROSPACE MARINE AND DEFENSE MARKETS ARE REFLECTED IN THE QUALITY CRITERIA USED BY VICKERS.

Lightweight components made by Vickers provide efficient fluid power aboard compact commuter aircraft. Military aerospace applications include bomber planes, helicopters, and missiles.

Vickers fluid power components are integral to power and motion control systems aboard ships and submarines, as well as in dockside and offshore installations. Vickers components are found on aircraft carriers, attack and ballistic missile submarines, and the Aegis Class cruiser, as well as in weapons and torpedo propulsion systems.

Virtually every land-based defense vehicle that uses hydraulics relies on Vickers components. The company's American and European defense vehicle programs include rocket launchers, air defense systems, tanks, and support vehicles, including construction vehicles and personnel carriers. With the industry's most advanced research and development facilities and skilled personnel, Vickers is also the world leader in the design and development of new products for the aerospace, marine, and defense markets.

WORLD-CLASS FACILITIES

The Vickers Fluid Power Division operates world-class manufacturing facilities in the United States, United Kingdom, and Germany. The latest manufacturing processes and equipment allow Vickers to respond quickly and economically to customer needs.

The stringent quality and reliability standards of the aerospace, marine, and defense markets are reflected in the exacting quality criteria used by Vickers. The company's worldwide manufacturing operations in Jackson house more than 60,000 square feet of state-of-the-art testing facilities.

Superior customer service is a Vickers hallmark. Every Vickers product sold is serviced for life. Vickers and its affiliates operate 24-hour repair service centers in North America, Europe, and Japan. Regular customer support visits identify and correct potential problems, enhancing product reliability and extending product life.

The company's major manufacturing and service centers in the United States, United Kingdom,

Germany, and Asia are supported by a worldwide network of sales and service offices. The strategic locations of the company's facilities throughout the world ensure quick response to customer needs, no matter where the customer is located. Every 18 months, Vickers sponsors the International Aerospace Power and Motion Control Conference, which brings Vickers customers and suppliers together in a single forum to discuss the design, operation, and performance of Vickers products.

With a solid track record, more than 75 years of experience, and the vision to meet the rigorous demands of the next generation of aerospace, marine, and defense applications, Vickers remains the global fluid power and fuel pump products leader.

CLOCKWISE FROM TOP LEFT:
A SERIES OF INLINE PUMPS PROVIDE HYDRAULIC POWER FOR COMMERCIAL AND MILITARY AIRCRAFT.

THE AC ELECTRIC-MOTOR-DRIVEN PUMP PROVIDES AUXILIARY HYDRAULIC POWER FOR GROUND OPERATION ON BOARD COMMERCIAL AIRCRAFT.

THE VICKERS INTELLIGENT MOTOR™ IS A SOFTWARE-CONTROLLED, VARIABLE DISPLACEMENT HYDRAULIC MOTOR.

THE AUXILIARY POWER UNIT PUMP PROVIDES EMERGENCY POWER ON THE LOCKHEED MARTIN/BOEING F-22.

CHEMFIRST INC.

EADQUARTERED IN JACKSON, CHEMFIRST INC. IS A WORLD LEADER IN CHEMICAL manufacturing. The company, through its subsidiaries—First Chemical Corporation; Quality Chemicals, Inc. (QCI); EKC Technology, Inc.; TriQuest, LP; and Callidus Technologies Inc.—operates modern manufacturing facilities in six states and in Scotland. ChemFirst companies produce specialty chemicals and chemical intermediates for industry and agriculture, and provide engineered

products and services for chemical and other industries worldwide.

The ChemFirst operating units are leaders in their respective businesses. First Chemical Corporation produces chemical intermediates and specialty and performance chemicals for major chemical companies worldwide. QCI custom manufactures fine chemicals using both proprietary and customer-developed technology. EKC Technology is a leading manufacturer of advanced cleaning chemicals and chemical mechanical planarization (CMP) slurries for the manufacture of integrated circuits. TriQuest develops and markets deep ultraviolet (DUV) photoresists, which enable integrated circuit fabrication at or below .25-micron resolution, and other products. Callidus Technologies provides engineered products and services to chemical, steel, and other industries.

A FAVORITE WITH SHAREHOLDERS

ChemFirst has long been respected by investors and market analysts. In 1975, the company—then known as First Mississippi—became the first Mississippi-chartered company to be

listed on the New York Stock Exchange. *Money* magazine named the company a stock winner for the decade of the 1970s, with the biggest 10-year gain (1,725 percent) among 2,200 stocks traded on the New York and American exchanges and 830 major over-the-counter stocks.

For the five-year period that ended December 31, 1997, ChemFirst's revenue growth rate was 18 percent. Total return to shareholders for the same period was 631 percent compared to 151 percent for the Standard and Poor's 500. Sixteen percent of the company's stock is owned by ChemFirst employees.

"Our strategy is to grow our business by building on, adding to, and extending our technology base and market position," says J. Kelley Williams, ChemFirst's chairman and chief executive officer. "ChemFirst's focus is on products and services with high-margin and high-growth potential, and emphasis on technology. Our objective is to increase shareholder value."

FIRST CAME FERTILIZER

Chartered as First Mississippi Corporation in 1957, the company was founded as a venture capital firm to bring businesses to Mississippi. It later became known as a major fertilizer producer. The company moved into the chemicals business with the 1967 start-up of First Chemical Corp. in Pascagoula, Mississippi. The company further expanded its chemical operations with the 1986 purchase of Quality Chemicals, Inc. (QCI), a custom chemical manufacturer, and the 1989 acquisition of EKC Technology, Inc., an electronic chemicals business. The company acquired Plasma Energy Corporation in 1983 and started Callidus Technologies Inc. in 1989. These two companies provide engineered products and services to

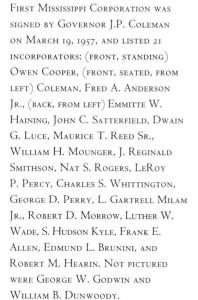

HEADQUARTERED IN JACKSON, CHEMFIRST INC. IS A WORLD LEADER IN CHEMICAL MANUFACTURING.

THE CHARTER OF INCORPORATION OF FIRST MISSISSIPPI CORPORATION WAS SIGNED BY GOVERNOR J.P. COLEMAN ON MARCH 19, 1957, AND LISTED 21 INCORPORATORS: (FRONT, STANDING) OWEN COOPER, (FRONT, SEATED, FROM LEFT) COLEMAN, FRED A. ANDERSON JR., (BACK, FROM LEFT) EMMITTE W. HAINING, JOHN C. SATTERFIELD, DWAIN G. LUCE, MAURICE T. REED SR., WILLIAM H. MOUNGER, J. REGINALD SMITHSON, NAT S. ROGERS, LEROY P. PERCY, CHARLES S. WHITTINGTON, GEORGE D. PERRY, L. GARTRELL MILAM JR., ROBERT D. MORROW, LUTHER W. WADE, S. HUDSON KYLE, FRANK E. ALLEN, EDMUND L. BRUNINI, AND ROBERT M. HEARIN. NOT PICTURED WERE GEORGE W. GODWIN AND WILLIAM B. DUNWOODY.

FRANK NOONE

chemical, steel, and other industries, and were combined in 1997 to gain efficiency. Plasma Energy now operates as a product line within Callidus.

In December 1992, management initiated a major restructuring effort to simplify and position the company to take advantage of business strengths and growth opportunities in chemicals and related businesses. Restructuring efforts since 1992 include the disposition of unrelated or insignificant technology businesses, the sale of oil and gas assets, and the sale of a coal business in 1993; the spin-off of Getchell Gold (formerly FirstMiss Gold) in 1995; the sale of an aluminum dross processing business in 1997; and the sale of a biomass-to-energy business in 1998.

In December 1996, the company's chemicals and nonfertilizer businesses were spun off tax free to shareholders as ChemFirst Inc., a new debt-free, publicly traded company, and First Mississippi's fertilizer operations were acquired by Mississippi Chemical Corp. in a stock-for-stock merger.

In December 1997, ChemFirst completed three acquisitions that complement and extend the company's successful electronic and performance chemicals business. Two of the acquisitions are product lines of high-purity, ultrafine abrasives for the CMP step in the manufacture of integrated circuits. The other acquisition, which formed a newly created company called TriQuest, LP, manufactures and markets derivatives of 4-hydroxyacetophenone, including the polymers used in DUV photoresist applications for integrated circuits, polymer additives for plastics, and specialty additives for coatings and adhesives.

EXCEPTIONAL BUSINESS PRACTICES

The company is committed to achieving compliance excellence in all of its facilities. Currently, four facilities have ISO 9002 certification for high standards of quality management systems. One plant is also certified for ISO 9001, which covers product design systems. The company's custom chemical manufacturing plant in

Tyrone, Pennsylvania, has received ISO 14001 for environmental standards systems and procedures, and electronic chemicals operations in Glasgow, Scotland, have received BS7750 certification, the British Standards equivalent. The ISO 9000 benchmarks have become a world standard—and, in some cases, a requirement—for securing new business.

Custom manufacturing facilities at Dayton, Ohio, operate under cGMP (current Good Manufacturing Practices) standards for production of pharmaceutical or food-related chemicals.

First Chemical Corporation has twice received Bayer Corporation's Milestone Award for Best Performing Raw Materials Supplier and Monsanto's Supplier Quality Recognition Award.

ENVIRONMENTAL AWARENESS

Environmental and community responsibility and employee health and safety are a top priority at ChemFirst. Participation in the U.S. Environmental Protection Agency's (EPA) 33/50 program won ChemFirst the Vice President's Hammer Award, which recognizes the company's participation in a voluntary program to reduce environmental releases of certain chemicals.

ChemFirst companies endorse and are actively implementing the Chemical Manufacturers Association's Responsible Care® initiative, a multistep discipline to continuously improve performance in health, safety, and environmental protection.

COMMUNITY SUPPORT

Funded by a percentage of the company's annual profits, the ChemFirst Inc. Foundation supports education, the arts, and conservation efforts. Over the years, the foundation has donated approximately $6 million to education, community service projects, and other charitable causes. ChemFirst's operating units are also strong supporters of local charities, schools, and civic groups in the individual communities where they operate.

"ChemFirst has built excellent working relationships with residents and local officials in every city in which we operate a facility," Williams says. "Through the continued support of our communities, our employees, and our customers, ChemFirst will build the trust necessary to grow and to create additional value for its shareholders."

CHEMFIRST IS COMMITTED TO ACHIEVING COMPLIANCE EXCELLENCE IN ALL OF ITS FACILITIES.

MISSISSIPPI VALLEY GAS COMPANY, THE LARGEST PRIVATELY OWNED NATURAL gas distribution company in the United States, provides safe, reliable service to more than 250,000 customers in more than 100 Mississippi communities. The company, founded in 1951, operates more than 5,000 miles of natural gas pipeline stretching through 33 Mississippi counties, serving residential, commercial, industrial, and governmental customers.

AFFORDABLE SERVICE, NEW TECHNOLOGIES

Surveys consistently show Mississippi Valley Gas customers' rates as among the lowest in the nation. The company also offers the convenience of a budget billing plan, which allows customers to prorate their gas consumption costs over a 12-month period, rather than face bills that fluctuate widely with the changing seasons. Customers may also purchase efficient, clean-burning natural gas appliances from Mississippi Valley Gas through installment payments, which are added to their monthly gas bills.

Mississippi Valley Gas is currently involved in the development of a number of new natural gas technologies. Research into natural gas air-conditioning and new desiccant systems, which remove high levels of humidity from the air, will result in an even greater level of comfort and cost savings for the company's customers.

GASMARK® HOMES

To help its customers further lower their utility costs and conserve energy, Mississippi Valley Gas developed the highly acclaimed GASMARK® program. GASMARK Homes are built from the ground up to ensure energy efficiency. GASMARK Homes feature special insulation, double-pane windows, gas appliances, and other amenities designed specifically to produce substantial energy savings.

Through the program, builders must meet stringent requirements regarding insulation, air infiltration, attic ventilation, and appliance efficiencies. Each home must undergo an approval process and is subsequently numbered and certified as a GASMARK Home for the benefit of future home buyers. GASMARK designs meet or exceed the American Society of Heating, Refrigeration, and Air-Conditioning Engineers, Inc. (ASHRAE) Standard 90—the benchmark by which all energy-efficient designs are measured.

FUELING MISSISSIPPI'S GROWTH

Both the affordability of natural gas and the state-of-the-art delivery infrastructure provided by Mississippi Valley Gas support business, industrial, and residential development in the 33 counties served by the company. Working in partnership with chambers of commerce, economic development organizations, and local officials, Mississippi Valley Gas recruits new businesses and industries, and brings new jobs into the local economy. The company's progressive industrial expansion policies encourage further economic growth throughout the Mississippi Valley Gas service area.

SERVICE TO THE COMMUNITY

Mississippi Valley Gas has a long-standing history of service to the Jackson area. The company and its 700 employees invest their time and energy in a number of community enrichment programs, including Adopt-A-School, Habitat for Humanity, the United Way, and the Salvation Army.

Through its continued dedication to its customers and the community it serves, Mississippi Valley Gas Company is poised to meet the future.

MISSISSIPPI VALLEY GAS COMPANY OPERATES MORE THAN 5,000 MILES OF NATURAL GAS PIPELINE STRETCHING THROUGH 33 MISSISSIPPI COUNTIES, SERVING RESIDENTIAL, COMMERCIAL, INDUSTRIAL, AND GOVERNMENTAL CUSTOMERS.

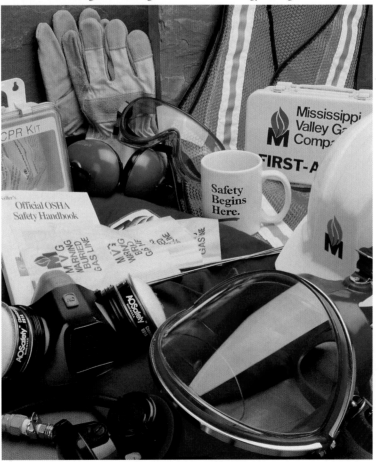

JACKSON

1959 - 1995

H OME TO 1,500 STUDENTS FROM PREKINDERGARTEN THROUGH 12TH GRADE, Jackson Academy (JA) is Mississippi's largest independent day school and one of the South's leading educational institutions. Founded in 1959, the school has built such a tradition of academic excellence and strong core values that often JA receives calls from new parents, still at hospitals, requesting to register their newborns for future enrollment. ✳ JA students benefit from an outstanding faculty and state-of-

the-art facilities. Approximately 60 percent of the school's caring and committed faculty hold advanced degrees. JA's 38-acre campus in the heart of Jackson includes a 20,000-square-foot learning center that features a state-of-the-art, automated library; a multimedia room; a foreign language department; and a 36-terminal computer lab. With campuswide networking and Internet access, the technologically advanced school also includes a 25-station elementary computer lab. Notably, Jackson Academy is one of only four schools in Mississippi to gain membership in the prestigious National Association of Independent Schools.

"JA stresses a traditional approach to curriculum, incorporating innovative concepts that stimulate enthusiasm for learning," says Headmaster Peter Jernberg. "In addition, emphasis on critical thinking, rather than simple memorization, ensures that JA students build the thinking and reasoning skills that allow them to excel not only in college, but also in the professional world."

The value of a JA education is best demonstrated by the outstanding achievements of the school's students. Within a 12-month period, two JA students scored perfect 1600s on the Scholastic Aptitude Test (SAT)—a feat accomplished by only seven of every 10,000 students nationwide. On average, 10 percent of JA seniors are recognized as National Merit Semifinalists.

JA students can enroll in 10 college-level advanced placement (AP) courses. These students perform well above the national average on AP exams, with some earning as much as a year of college credit.

Each year, JA graduates receive scholarship offers in excess of $1 million, and gain admission to the nation's most selective colleges and universities. In recent years, more than half of JA's graduates have received scholarships, with more than 10 percent receiving full-tuition awards. Colleges seek the well-rounded JA students who pursue a variety of interests in academic areas, as well as in athletics, fine arts, lead-

ership, and community service. JA students participate in student government; stage dramatic performances; write for the school literary magazine; join the marching band, chorus, or dance team; compete in superior athletic programs; and participate in dozens of other special-interest organizations.

A Values-Oriented Environment

Equally as critical as academics is the JA focus on relationships. "JA enjoys a rich tradition of serving families with a commitment to superior educational opportunities in a student-centered environment," Jernberg says. "Our family atmosphere has long been a distinguishing feature of Jackson Academy."

Calvin Thigpen—former JA valedictorian, student body president at JA and later at the University of Mississippi, and recipient of the prestigious University of Mississippi Newman Scholarship—summarized the uniqueness of Jackson Academy in his class day address. He said, "The parents and students share a bond of love and support. The students and faculty share a bond of cooperation and friendship. The faculty and parents share a bond of understanding and appreciation. Together, the three groups comprise the Jackson Academy family, a union of people closer than you will find at any other institution."

CLOCKWISE FROM TOP LEFT: "JA [JACKSON ACADEMY] STRESSES A TRADITIONAL APPROACH TO CURRICULUM, INCORPORATING INNOVATIVE CONCEPTS THAT STIMULATE ENTHUSIASM FOR LEARNING," SAYS HEADMASTER PETER JERNBERG. "IN ADDITION, EMPHASIS ON CRITICAL THINKING, RATHER THAN SIMPLE MEMORIZATION, ENSURES THAT JA STUDENTS BUILD THE THINKING AND REASONING SKILLS THAT ALLOW THEM TO EXCEL NOT ONLY IN COLLEGE, BUT ALSO IN THE PROFESSIONAL WORLD."

JACKSON ACADEMY STUDENTS BENEFIT FROM AN OUTSTANDING FACULTY AND STATE-OF-THE-ART FACILITIES.

JA STUDENTS PARTICIPATE IN STUDENT GOVERNMENT; STAGE DRAMATIC PERFORMANCES; WRITE FOR THE SCHOOL LITERARY MAGAZINE; JOIN THE MARCHING BAND, CHORUS, OR DANCE TEAM; COMPETE IN SUPERIOR ATHLETIC PROGRAMS; AND PARTICIPATE IN DOZENS OF OTHER SPECIAL-INTEREST ORGANIZATIONS.

Brown's Fine Art & Framing, Inc.

Mississippi recognizes itself as a significant contributor to the fine arts. As an active local promoter of this reputation, Brown's Fine Art & Framing showcases paintings, carvings, and pottery by Mississippi artists, as well as works by national and international talents. Exquisite originals by Emmitt Thames, James Josey, Sharon Richardson, and Jackie Meena, as well as works by dozens of other gifted artists, adorn the walls of the eclectic gallery on Fondren Place.

A Colorful History

Brown's Fine Art & Framing entered the Jackson art scene in 1965, when Mary Grace and James Brown opened a small frame shop on North State Street. Initially, James kept his job during the day at the Swift and Company Meat Packing Plant, and cut and joined frames by night. A pioneer in the professional custom-framing industry, Brown's Fine Art & Framing became an essential aspect of the growing Jackson art market. "When you're in the framing business, you're automatically in the art business," Brown often remarked during his lifetime. "Everything you frame is an artwork in and of itself." And with an increasing number of serious collectors bringing art in for framing, the Browns recognized the potential for a fine art gallery in the capital city.

In 1970, Brown's Fine Art & Framing held its first major opening, a showing of works by Thames, a Mississippi painter. Since then, the gallery has led the way in introducing new artists to Mississippi collectors and promoting Mississippi artists to the rest of the country. Today, Brown's Fine Art & Framing is owned and operated by Mary Grace Brown and her children, Allison Brown Simmons and Joel Brown, who are committed to continuing the shop's artistic tradition.

Mississippi in the National Spotlight

Mississippi's artistic community achieved national recognition during the gallery's 1989 tribute to legendary Jackson writer Eudora Welty. Brown's Fine Art & Framing asked its artists to create works based on Welty's writings, and donated a portion of the proceeds to the Welty Library in downtown Jackson. The gallery raised enough money to become a major underwriter of the library's Mississippi Writers Room. The show and its artists received national media coverage, and the gallery won the Award of Excellence from *Decor* magazine, the picture framing and art industry's trade magazine.

"The Welty show encompassed everything Brown's is about," says Joel Brown. "It brought our artists national acclaim, tied in the educational side with paintings of literary works, contributed to a good cause, and spotlighted Eudora Welty, who is a national treasure. And as an added bonus, it brought us many new customers."

Today, Brown's Fine Art & Framing attracts art enthusiasts from throughout Mississippi and the Southeast. Walter Anderson's painted silk screens, the Mississippi Duck Stamp print, and works by other Mississippi artists are sold to collectors as far away as New York; Washington, D.C.; California Montana; and Alaska. Making an impact at home, Brown's Fine Art & Framing has donated artwork and show proceeds to a number of local charities. In 1997, the Metro Jackson Chamber of Commerce presented the gallery with the Award of Excellence for Small Business.

"We hope to continue representing the best artists and offering the finest framing in Jackson for generations to come," Mary Grace Brown says. "It thrills us to see customers who were with us in the beginning coming back and introducing their children and grandchildren to fine art at Brown's."

TODAY, BROWN'S FINE ART & FRAMING IS OWNED AND OPERATED BY MARY GRACE BROWN AND HER CHILDREN, ALLISON BROWN SIMMONS AND JOEL BROWN, WHO ARE COMMITTED TO CONTINUING THE SHOP'S ARTISTIC TRADITION.

KLLM Transport Services, Inc.

ONE OF THE NATION'S LARGEST TRUCKLOAD CARRIERS OF TEMPERATURE-controlled commodities, KLLM Transport Services, Inc. provides efficient, reliable transportation throughout North America. KLLM derives about 70 percent of its revenues from hauling temperature-controlled commodities, including food, medical supplies, and specialty chemicals. In addition, the company transports dry goods, and further

CLOCKWISE FROM TOP LEFT:
W.J. "BILLY" LILES (LEFT) AND B.C.
"BENNY" LEE COFOUNDED KLLM.

STEVE BEVILAQUA SERVES AS KLLM'S
PRESIDENT AND CEO.

TODAY, KLLM'S FLEET INCLUDES
MORE THAN 1,800 TRACTORS AND 2,800
TEMPERATURE-CONTROLLED TRAILERS.

VERNON SAWYER IS A KLLM SUBSIDIARY.

expanded its dry transport services with the 1995 acquisition of Vernon Sawyer, a highly successful dry freight operator based in Louisiana.

A number of Fortune 500 companies rely on KLLM for safe shipping and dependable, on-time delivery. The company's impressive client list includes Procter & Gamble, Pillsbury, Kroger, Fresh Express, and Union Carbide. "Our commitment to our customers and to our shareholders is the same," says Steve Bevilaqua, KLLM president and CEO. "We provide the absolute best, most reliable service in the industry."

The Long Road to the Top

When KLLM opened for business in 1963, "headquarters" was the back room of a Phillips 66 station on Highway 80. The company was founded by four partners: Tom Kobuke, W.J. "Billy" Liles, B.C. "Benny" Lee, and Henry Moudy. The name KLLM is an acronym derived from the initials of each partner's last name.

Ask Lee, current KLLM chairman of the board, why the four went into business together, and his answer is simple: "We were broke. I was in the poultry business and Billy [Liles] was in wholesale produce. It just made sense to start a brokerage business."

The first KLLM trucks went out with chickens and came back with produce. At that time, Liles was KLLM's only full-time employee. The staff doubled when the company hired a combination book-keeper and general office clerk, then tripled when a dispatcher came aboard to book loads and secure trucks.

KLLM bought its first truck in 1966. A year later, that "very used" Mack was traded in on the company's first new tractor, a brand-new Freight-liner. KLLM hasn't stopped growing since. Today, the company's fleet includes more than 1,800 tractors and 2,800 temperature-controlled trailers. KLLM operates terminals in Mississippi, Louisiana, California, Georgia, Pennsylvania, and Illinois, and employs more than 2,200 people, coordinating operations from its corporate headquarters in Jackson.

The company's annual gross sales exceed $300 million and are growing. KLLM is one of the largest temperature-controlled carriers in North America. In 1986, KLLM went public, but Liles and Lee retained principal ownership of the company they founded.

In It for the Long Haul

Continuous investment in the best technology, equipment, and people helps KLLM maintain its leadership position and improve on its already impressive 98 percent on-time delivery rate.

KLLM leads the industry in the use of high technology to enhance operations. The firm was the first temperature-controlled trucking company to use a computer-satellite communications system to link its fleet with the company headquarters. This system allows constant tracking of every truck in the fleet, and two-way communication between drivers and dispatchers 24 hours a day. The system ensures the safety of drivers and their cargo, and allows KLLM to provide customers with exact-to-the-minute delivery times.

To ensure its fleet is always running in top condition, KLLM inspects its own trucks and operates its own maintenance facilities. The firm also focuses on recruiting and retaining the industry's best drivers, and receives mail every month from satisfied customers praising the hardworking, conscientious individuals who represent KLLM on the road.

"Expanding the company involves more than buying trucks," Bevilaqua says. "You have to have good people to drive them and to perform in accordance with customer expectations. Our drivers know that if they satisfy our customers, they have a bright future with KLLM."

Outstanding Customer Service

Judging from their track records with the company, KLLM customers are very satisfied indeed. For example, Kroger has been a KLLM customer for 30 years, and Pillsbury has shipped with KLLM for 15 years. "When you're with a company that long, you're ingrained in their distribution pro-cess," Bevilaqua says. "They rely on you to get the job done just as surely as they rely on their own people." Building these long-term relationships with high-caliber customers is the key to the company's growth. Major corporations with multiple locations and high-volume shipping needs are the ideal KLLM customer.

"KLLM works best with companies that are interested in building partnerships, are willing to pay a fair price for superior service, and have the potential for growth," Bevilaqua says. "KLLM always works to keep the price as low as possible, but we will always emphasize superior service over cutting costs. Our customers know they can rely on KLLM for on-time pickup and delivery, billing accuracy, and merchandise that arrives in good condition. When companies put their business in our hands, they know they can count on KLLM to deliver."

METHODIST HEALTHCARE

SINCE 1965, METHODIST HEALTHCARE-JACKSON HOSPITALS, AN AFFILIATE OF Memphis-based Methodist Healthcare, has fulfilled its pledge to treat patients responsibly, effectively, and with a reverence for the miracle of life. Methodist Healthcare is a network of 15 hospitals in Mississippi and Tennessee, and is owned by the Memphis, Mississippi, and Arkansas conferences of the United Methodist Church. Methodist Healthcare's 2,300 physicians, nurses, and medical and professional staff members in the Mississippi Division are committed to providing advanced, cost-effective, compassionate health care that reflects the Christian mission and social principles of the United Methodist Church.

The Methodist Healthcare-Main Campus on Chadwick Drive in Jackson serves as a referral center for Methodist Healthcare-North Campus—also located in Jackson—and for Methodist Healthcare-Middle Mississippi Campus, an 84-bed facility in Lexington. Through its network of hospitals and clinics, Methodist makes outstanding health care convenient and accessible to all of Jackson and central Mississippi.

COMPREHENSIVE MEDICAL CARE AND SERVICES

The flagship of Methodist Healthcare's Mississippi Division is the 409-bed hospital on the Main Campus. Every major medical specialty is represented on the hospital's staff, which includes more than 330 respected physicians.

More than 25,000 procedures are performed each year through the Methodist Healthcare-Cancer Care program. Methodist is the only private facility in central Mississippi to offer stereotactic radiosurgery, a breakthrough procedure that uses a single dose of radiation to treat brain tumors.

The Methodist Healthcare-Cardiac Care Center offers complete diagnostic and therapeutic care for every known heart disorder. Invasive and noninvasive procedures, including cardiac catheterization, balloon angioplasty, and open-heart surgery are performed by Methodist's renowned cardiac care experts.

Each year, more than 1,500 babies are delivered at the Maternity Center at Methodist Healthcare. The center offers eight spacious labor/delivery/recovery suites that combine modern medical technology with the comforts of home. When special infant care is needed, assistance is only steps from the delivery room. The center has

CLOCKWISE FROM TOP:
METHODIST HEALTHCARE REMAINS TRUE TO ITS MISSION OF PROVIDING EXCEPTIONAL HEALTH CARE WELL WITHIN THE REACH OF THOSE IN NEED.

METHODIST HEALTHCARE IS A NETWORK OF 15 HOSPITALS IN MISSISSIPPI AND TENNESSEE, AND IS OWNED BY THE MEMPHIS, MISSISSIPPI, AND ARKANSAS CONFERENCES OF THE UNITED METHODIST CHURCH.

THROUGH ITS NETWORK OF HOSPITALS AND CLINICS, METHODIST MAKES OUTSTANDING HEALTH CARE CONVENIENT AND ACCESSIBLE TO ALL OF JACKSON AND CENTRAL MISSISSIPPI.

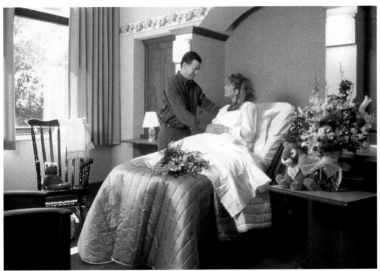

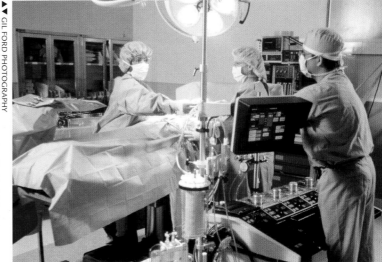

one of Mississippi's largest neonatal intensive care units, which is staffed by five neonatologists.

The Sleep Disorders Center at Methodist Healthcare provides monitoring and therapies for patients suffering from narcolepsy, insomnia, sleepwalking, nightmares, and other disorders that prevent a good night's sleep.

Housed within a local YMCA, the Methodist Healthcare-Rehabilitative Services Outpatient Therapy Center is equipped with the most advanced technology and staffed by therapists experienced in rehabilitating cardiac and stroke patients, as well as workers suffering from job-related injuries. The center houses Mississippi's only Primus machine, a device that simulates activities such as driving, shoveling, and lifting, and that measures patients' progress at performing these tasks. The Outpatient Therapy Center also has a model of a house, designed specifically to provide work-hardening experience in order to rehabilitate painters, carpenters, and electricians injured on the job.

The Methodist Healthcare-Main Campus continues to enhance the services it provides to patients by investing in the latest technological advances and by working to maintain high levels of patient satisfaction.

METHODIST HEALTHCARE-NORTH CAMPUS

Opened in 1996, Methodist Healthcare-North Campus provides convenient care for the rapidly growing population of north Jackson and adjacent Madison County. The $27 million, 64-bed facility offers general medical and surgical procedures, diagnostic services, plastic surgery, radiology, obstetrics, pediatrics, neurology, and general medical care. The Methodist Healthcare-North Campus also includes a minor emergency clinic, outpatient center, and medical/surgical unit. Its special Women's Center features seven labor/delivery/recovery/postpartum (LDRP) suites and a well baby nursery.

Methodist Healthcare-North Campus also offers free health screenings, health- and wellness-related seminars, and classes on topics ranging from childbirth to CPR. In addition to the hospital's services, community members have convenient access to medical specialists who practice in an adjoining medical office building.

PRIMARY AND SPECIALTY CARE CLINICS

Methodist's growing network of primary and specialty care clinics puts quality health care within reach of residents throughout central Mississippi. These facilities include Methodist Healthcare-Family Care Centers—a network of primary care clinics with locations in Carthage, Clinton, Ridgeland, and Crystal Springs—and the Methodist Healthcare-Family Care Center in Kosciusko.

Specialty care clinics include Methodist Healthcare Neuroscience Associates, for treatment of injuries and disorders of the brain and spinal cord; Methodist Healthcare-Orthopaedic Associates, providing care for injuries, such as sprains and fractures, and more specialized treatment, such as hip and knee replacements; and Methodist Healthcare-Internal Medicine Associates.

Methodist Healthcare is also a leader in providing home health care to patients requiring quality long-term care, eliminating the expense of a lengthy hospital stay. Its Home Care Services program delivers a variety of specialized hospital services directly to patients' homes. In addition, Methodist Healthcare-Home Medical Equipment provides the equipment and supplies needed by homebound patients.

HEALTH CHOICE OF MISSISSIPPI

Methodist was the first hospital in Mississippi to offer a hospital-based managed care program. Health Choice of Mississippi is a unique partnership between doctors and health care professionals who have joined with Methodist Healthcare to contain costs while improving access to health care.

Comprising three hospitals, a home health agency, five family care centers, and four specialty clinics, and having plans to expand throughout central Mississippi in the near future, Methodist Healthcare remains true to its mission of providing exceptional health care well within the reach of those in need.

EACH YEAR, MORE THAN 1,500 BABIES ARE DELIVERED AT THE MATERNITY CENTER, WHICH OFFERS EIGHT SPACIOUS LABOR/DELIVERY/RECOVERY SUITES THAT COMBINE MODERN MEDICAL TECHNOLOGY WITH THE COMFORTS OF HOME (LEFT).

INVASIVE AND NONINVASIVE PROCEDURES, INCLUDING CARDIAC CATHETERIZATION, BALLOON ANGIOPLASTY, AND OPEN-HEART SURGERY, ARE PERFORMED BY METHODIST'S RENOWNED CARDIAC CARE EXPERTS (RIGHT).

KEY CONSTRUCTORS, INC.

EVERY JACKSONIAN WHO HAS NAVIGATED THE STACK, THE MONOLITH OF interstate construction linking Interstates 55 and 20, benefits from the expertise of Key Constructors. A general contracting firm specializing in highway and heavy construction, Key Constructors has been building bridges, overpasses, dams, culverts, and levies since 1975. Specializing in construction that involves concrete and structural steel erection, the company's projects may never be described as glamorous, but they are vital in keeping Jackson moving.

UNDER CONSTRUCTION
"We're a steady company," says Charles Webster, owner and president. "We pride ourselves on doing good work in a timely manner and staying within the budget." And some of those budgets can be staggering. Key Constructors worked extensively on the $45 million Stack, both as a subcontractor and as the prime contractor on the job.

As a subcontractor of APAC-Miss., the company also is handling the structural work involved in the widening of Lakeland Drive from St. Dominic Hospital to Airport Road, working at night to avoid the $100-per-minute penalty charged for lane closures during business hours. Recent projects outside Jackson proper included the construction of the Yazoo River Bridge at Highway 49 West, which carried a $10 million price tag, and the $18 million relocation of Highway 45 south of Tupelo.

Ninety-eight percent of the company's business is earned through a competitive bidding process. Key Constructors' clients include the Mississippi Department of Transportation, the Natural Resources Conservation Service (NRCS), and the Corps of Engineers. While the majority of the company's current work is in Mississippi, Key Constructors has also completed projects in Louisiana, Texas, and Arkansas.

A DISTINCTIVE ADDRESS
While Key Constructors didn't build it, the company is closely linked to another notable construction project. The firm is headquartered in a replicated antebellum mansion built personally by Charles Webster and his wife.

While on a tour of antebellum homes in Charleston, South Carolina, the Websters visited Drayton Hall, a Federal-style mansion built in 1738. Charles used the last two exposures left in his camera to photograph the exterior of the mansion. The elegant Madison County building that now houses Key Constructors and a handful of other tenants was replicated using those two snapshots as reference.

A FIRM FOUNDATION
In 1974, Charles Webster was president of Con-Plex, Inc., a Jackson-based general contracting and construction firm owned by U.S. Industries, a conglomerate of more than 118 companies

A GENERAL CONTRACTING FIRM SPECIALIZING IN HIGHWAY AND HEAVY CONSTRUCTION, KEY CONSTRUCTORS HAS BEEN BUILDING BRIDGES, OVERPASSES, DAMS, CULVERTS, AND LEVIES SINCE 1975.

worldwide. Webster had been with the company for more than 16 years when he decided to establish his own contracting business. "I had seen many sides of big business and was ready for a change," Webster recalls.

Three members of the Con-Plex senior staff—including the comptroller and chief engineer—decided Webster had the right idea. Joined by John Brown Humphreys, Tom Hendrix, and R.D. Bickerstaff, Charles Webster resigned his position and founded a new company. When one of his three business associates reminded Webster that "all the key people came with you," the new firm was christened Key Constructors.

The company's first client was the Tennessee Valley Authority, which hired Key Constructors to drive pilings for transmission lines in the backwaters of Enid Lake in Mississippi. "This was extremely dangerous work," Webster recalls. "We accepted the job not only because we were a new company hungry for business, but because we were young and foolish." Through this and other projects, Key Constructors quickly earned a solid reputation for good work, and was soon handling projects for clients throughout Mississippi, Louisiana, Arkansas, and Texas.

THE KEY TO SUCCESS

People are still the key to the company's success. Today, Key Constructors employs between 125 and 225 skilled workers, including seasonal construction workers. Many of the firm's permanent and managerial employees are following a family tradition. "We're proud to point to several second-generation employees, and even a few third-generation people on our team," Webster says. "Recruiting the best people is critical to the success of the business. It all goes back to the original 'key' concept."

The evolution following the death of R.D. Bickerstaff and retirement of J.B. Humphreys has made room for Paul McPhail, chief engineer/secretary, and David Trevathan, vice president of operations.

Charles Webster has also become a key leader in the construction industry, serving three terms on the board of directors of the Mississippi Road Builders Association and two terms as the association's president. "We're proud of the reputation Key Constructors has earned over the years," Webster says. "People recognize us as a straightforward, hardworking company conducting business with integrity."

SPECIALIZING IN CONSTRUCTION THAT INVOLVES CONCRETE AND STRUCTURAL STEEL ERECTION, THE COMPANY'S PROJECTS MAY NEVER BE DESCRIBED AS GLAMOROUS, BUT THEY ARE VITAL IN KEEPING JACKSON MOVING (TOP).

THE FIRM IS HEADQUARTERED IN A REPLICATED ANTEBELLUM MANSION BUILT PERSONALLY BY CHARLES WEBSTER AND HIS WIFE. THE ELEGANT MADISON COUNTY BUILDING NOW HOUSES KEY CONSTRUCTORS AND A HANDFUL OF OTHER TENANTS (BOTTOM).

A COMPANY OFTEN TAKES ON THE PERSONALITY OF ITS LEADER. THAT IS CERTAINLY the case with Byrd & Associates, a Jackson law firm with a reputation as a champion of the underdog and a force for social change. ✳ Founded by Isaac K. Byrd Jr., a nationally respected trial lawyer, Byrd & Associates has won several multimillion-dollar verdicts in landmark personal injury, medical malpractice, consumer fraud, and product liability cases. "We look for cases that can make

a difference," Byrd says. "This firm changes the way institutions respond to the needs of real people. When we win a case, we have usually made an institution accountable to human needs."

THE PRACTICE

Byrd & Associates' office grounds, often used for political and social functions, consist of an 1895 Victorian home and two other restored houses in a tree-lined section of town.

The six attorneys who comprise Byrd & Associates have tried cases involving everything from farming accidents to sexual harassment to swimming pool drowning, all with impressive results.

In 1987, Byrd, as cocounsel, won a $4.5 million medical malpractice verdict, at that time the largest actual damage verdict in Mississippi history. It was the first of many multimillion-dollar judgments and settlements for clients throughout the state. Portions of the profits from these verdicts help the firm litigate causes in which it believes; in 1998, the firm settled an eight-figure medical negligence suit. More than 20 percent of Byrd & Associates' work is handled pro bono.

While the firm tackles many controversial issues—and a few that are unpopular—Byrd & Associates is well respected by other Jackson businesses, including opposing counsels. "We believe in the causes for which we fight," Byrd says simply. "And people respect that. Besides, everyone likes a fighter." Oftentimes after serving in adversarial roles against the firm, business leaders or corporate attorneys seek out the firm to help litigate their personal cases.

THE FOUNDER

Byrd's influence extends well beyond the Jackson city limits. One of four African-Americans in the United States on the board of governors of the Association of Trial Lawyers of America (ATLA), the world's largest trial bar, he also serves on the boards of the Trial Lawyers for Public Justice, a national public interest law firm, and the National American Civil Liberties Union (ACLU). Byrd is general counsel to the Mississippi Conference NAACP, as well.

Valedictorian of his Indianola high school and magna cum laude graduate of Tougaloo College, Byrd earned his law degree from the Northwestern University School of Law, practiced in Chicago for two years, and then returned to Mississippi to, as he says, "help change the social, political, and legal fiber of my home state. There were opportunities to make a difference in Mississippi." His success at making a difference has earned Byrd countless awards from state and national professional and civic organizations, including the prestigious 1998 Goodman-Chaney-Schwerner Award, presented by the Mississippi Conference NAACP for promoting political empowerment for all citizens. In addition, he is an adjunct professor at Mississippi College of Law, where he teaches pretrial practice.

Establishing a foundation to fund educational and charitable causes, Byrd is a strong supporter of the arts, having served on the boards of the Arts Alliance, Mississippi Opera, New Stage Theatre, and Ballet Magnificat. He helped to spearhead fund-raising efforts for many community activities, including the Medgar Evers Statute Fund.

Byrd has also been a prominent player in Mississippi politics for more than two decades, but has never run for public office. When a chancery judge died in 1989, Governor Ray Mabus appointed Byrd to finish his term, making Byrd the first African-American chancery judge in Mississippi history. After holding the position for the remaining six months of the term, Byrd returned to his law practice rather than seek election to the position permanently. "My allegiance is always to my family and my law practice," Byrd says. "My commitment to changing Mississippi is larger than one office. Through this firm, I can wake up every day and make a difference."

FOUNDED BY ISAAC K. BYRD, JR., A NATIONALLY RESPECTED TRIAL LAWYER, BYRD & ASSOCIATES HAS WON SEVERAL MULTIMILLION-DOLLAR VERDICTS IN LANDMARK PERSONAL INJURY, MEDICAL MALPRACTICE, CONSUMER FRAUD, AND PRODUCT LIABILITY CASES (TOP).

THE OFFICE GROUNDS, OFTEN USED FOR MANY POLITICAL AND SOCIAL FUNCTIONS, CONSIST OF AN 1895 VICTORIAN HOME AND TWO OTHER RESTORED HOUSES ON A TREE-LINED SECTION OF TOWN (BOTTOM).

ISSISSIPPI'S ONLY STATEWIDE BUSINESS PUBLICATION, THE *Mississippi Business Journal (MBJ)* has covered the business beat since 1979. From the Memphis suburbs of DeSoto County to the booming Gulf Coast, the weekly *MBJ* is Mississippi's essential source for business news. ✳ "We strive to be an indispensable asset to our readers, many of whom are the leading decision makers in Mississippi business, industry, politics, and education," Owner and Publisher Joe D. Jones, CPA, explains. More than 65 percent of *MBJ*'s readers earn in excess of $50,000 annually and hold high-level positions in Mississippi's leading businesses. An impressive 92 percent of readers say they consider *MBJ* to be "the superior source of information for local business news."

"Our readers are well off, educated, and in positions of influence. They count on us to deliver timely business news in a format they can digest quickly and use on a daily basis," says Ronald Jones, general manager and stockholder. "Demographically, advertisers want to reach people like our readers. Our advertisers have found that *MBJ* is an excellent, affordable vehicle that speaks to their target markets."

INVESTING IN TECHNOLOGY

MBJ was one of the first newspapers in Mississippi to establish an Internet presence. The *MBJ* Web site at www.msbusiness.com is updated weekly and includes all of the information found in the printed edition. "We use the latest technology to deliver the latest business news to our readers," says Jim Laird, editor. "In addition to thousands of subscribers around the state, we've always had readers from different regions of the country. Now, we have readers from around the world. I get E-mail regularly from people reading us in Canada, South America, and Australia."

SPECIAL PUBLICATIONS AND PROJECTS

MBJ's special publications department creates new products for targeted audiences, including *Mississippi Investor*, *Construction Mississippi*, and most recently, the *Pine Belt Business Journal*. In addition, *MBJ* hosts the state's largest business-to-business trade show, the Mississippi Business EXPO. Held every January at the Trade Mart in Jackson, EXPO showcases hundreds of exhibitors and is attended by thousands of businesspeople. "Other shows have tried to compete, but none have experienced the success that EXPO enjoys," says Publisher Joe D. Jones, CPA. "I think *MBJ*'s reputation and involvement have played a crucial role in the show's popularity."

LEADING WITH ENTHUSIASM AND INTEGRITY

MBJ is known for balanced, fair, and comprehensive coverage of complex—and at times, controversial—issues. The paper has won many awards from the Mississippi Press Association (MPA), including overall excellence in its first year of MPA competition.

"We're proud of the accolades our hard work has earned from both our readers and our peers," Jones says. "I'm humbled by the many letters and phone calls I receive thanking us for a story or a column we've run. We play a vital role in the state's economic success, and we do everything we can to ensure that Mississippians take advantage of the tremendous potential here. Ultimately, that's our goal at the *Mississippi Business Journal*."

LEFT: Two *Mississippi Business Journal* STAFFERS DISCUSS AN UPCOMING ISSUE.

RIGHT: *Mississippi Business Journal*'S MANAGEMENT TEAM INCLUDES (FROM LEFT) ABBY ASKIN-BULLARD, DIRECTOR OF SPECIAL PUBLICATIONS; KAREN GILDER, ADVERTISING DIRECTOR; JOE D. JONES, CPA, PUBLISHER; RONALD JONES, GENERAL MANAGER; AND JIM LAIRD, EDITOR.

SHANNON SHERIDAN/SHERIDAN PHOTOGRAPHY

Waste Management is an international company that provides environmentally safe waste disposal and recycling services to communities worldwide. With more than $9 billion in annual revenue, Waste Management is the largest company of its kind in the world. The company's Jackson operation, Waste Management of Mississippi-Jackson, provides waste removal service for 60,000 business and residential customers in the Jackson

metropolitan area, offering a single source for questions, comments, and problem resolution.

Through its commercial and industrial collection service, Waste Management serves hospitals, retail shops, apartments, airports, shopping centers, schools, the leasing of portable sanitation facilities (Port-O-Lets), and other services with waste collec-

tion containers. The types and sizes of containers, as well as the frequency of collection, are tailored to each customer's needs.

The residential section provides a solid waste collection program that matches labor and equipment to the population, geography, and waste-generating characteristics of the area. Curbside collection and back-door pickup are two services frequently provided under contracts with municipal governments and/or individual home owners.

CLEANING UP JACKSON AND MISSISSIPPI

Waste Management of Mississippi-Jackson began operations in the capital city in 1978, providing efficient, affordable waste removal for business

and industrial clients. In 1986, the company won the City of Jackson's residential contract in a competitive bidding process. Waste Management has provided reliable curbside trash pickup for the residents of Jackson ever since, renewing its contract in 1992 and in 1997.

"Winning and renewing the City of Jackson's residential contract is the accomplishment we're most proud of," says Woody Wilson, Jackson division president and general manager. "The city gave Waste Management the opportunity to prove that we could provide cost-effective, efficient, environmentally friendly service, and we've done just that since 1986. The key to retaining the city's business has been and continues to be exceptional service for our customers."

As part of the new contract with the city, Waste Management provides—without additional charge—roll-off containers to each ward of the city once a month for the collection of trash and bulky waste. Waste Management is committed to a lasting partnership with the City of Jackson.

ECONOMIC IMPACT
Waste Management of Central Mississippi's Jackson Collection and Recycling Facility packs a strong economic punch in Jackson and Hinds County. Waste Management employs some 150 workers in the Jackson area, with a local annual payroll in excess of $5.3 million. The company spends more than $5 million in local purchases and contributes more than $134,000 annually in Hinds County real estate, personal property, and vehicle taxes.

Including the service it provides in Jackson, Waste Management has a 40 to 50 percent share of the waste disposal market in Mississippi. The company provides services in all 82 counties and has sales statewide topping $100 million.

"We will invest in the community through education, civic, cultural, and other charitable support, and will encourage employee involvement and leadership in community organizations

and projects," says Wilson. "We review every opportunity to hire qualified people from the local community. Additionally, we will work toward employing a more diverse workforce representative of the local population."

COMMUNITY CONTRIBUTIONS AND INVOLVEMENT
Waste Management's Jackson division makes annual cash and in-kind service contributions to a number of central Mississippi activities and events, including the Madison Central High School Booster Club, Westside Community Picnic, Rankin County Human Resource Agency, Jackson Rotary Club Charities, Inc., Central Mississippi Growth Foundation Youth Summit, Deposit Guaranty Golf Classic, Mississippi City and County Management Association, Jackson State University, and Mississippi State University. The company is also a major supporter of the United Way, the United Negro College Fund, the and National Association for the Advancement of Colored People (NAACP).

Waste Management holds membership in the Brandon, Madison,

Clinton, Metro Jackson, Ridgeland, and Pearl chambers of commerce, and is also involved in a number of community enhancement programs with an environmental slant, including Keep Jackson Beautiful.

"Waste management continues to be a leader not only in the environmental industry, but in the communities where the company operates, as well," Wilson says. "Our vision is to be the number one company in the industry, not only in terms of size and sales, but also in customer service and community enhancement."

INCLUDING THE SERVICE IT PROVIDES IN JACKSON, WASTE MANAGEMENT HAS A 40 TO 50 PERCENT SHARE OF THE WASTE DISPOSAL MARKET IN MISSISSIPPI. THE COMPANY PROVIDES SERVICES IN ALL 82 COUNTIES AND HAS SALES STATEWIDE TOPPING $100 MILLION.

MATTIACE PROPERTIES, INC.

FROM THE TURN OF THE CENTURY THROUGH THE EARLY 1970S, DOWNTOWN Jackson's Capitol Street was the retail corridor in Jackson. First, suburban shopping centers began popping up in outlying neighborhoods. Then, Jackson's first regional mall opened in central Jackson, which operated until Metro Center Mall opened in 1979. A new mall was added approximately six years later called Northpark. The explosion of complementary retail at both of these malls is due in part to the

work of Mattiace Properties, Inc. Jackson residents who shop at Target, PetSmart, Home Depot, or Office Depot can thank Mattiace Properties, Inc., for bringing these popular retailers to the Jackson area. Mattiace Properties is the largest retail development and management company in Mississippi. Since 1979, upscale shopping centers and office buildings developed and managed by Mattiace Properties have been constructed in Mississippi, Louisiana, and Tennessee, attracting tenants of the highest caliber.

In an average 12-month period, Mattiace Properties develops some 500,000 square feet of commercial real estate in the Southeast. Mattiace has constructed more than 1 million square feet of buildings, utilizing 140 acres of land in Jackson. These devel-

opments have created 1,500 full-time jobs and approximately 3,000 construction jobs. The completed projects have generated an estimated $15 million per year in sales tax revenue.

BRINGING MAJOR RETAILERS TO JACKSON

Mattiace Properties specializes in the development of shopping centers known in the industry as "community

power centers." Drawing consumers from a 10-mile radius, these centers are anchored by value-oriented retailers, most often a home improvement store like Home Depot or a variety discount store like Target or Wal-Mart.

"We start with the anchor store, then determine what would be complementary to that store. Next, we look at what consumers want and need that isn't already available in the area," explains Andrew Mattiace, the company's president and founder. "The end result is value and convenience in one location. Busy consumers can park at the front door, pick up what they need, and get in and out in a hurry."

The power strip concept is also popular among retailers who find rent and operating costs much lower than in a traditional, enclosed shop-

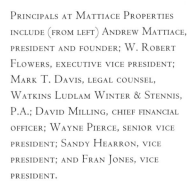

Mattiace Properties' largest undertaking to date has been the Junction Shopping Center at County Line Road and Interstate 55. The center features major retailers, such as Target and Home Depot.

Principals at Mattiace Properties include (from left) Andrew Mattiace, president and founder; W. Robert Flowers, executive vice president; Mark T. Davis, legal counsel, Watkins Ludlam Winter & Stennis, P.A.; David Milling, chief financial officer; Wayne Pierce, senior vice president; Sandy Hearron, vice president; and Fran Jones, vice president.

ping mall. Tenants save on common-area expenses found in malls, including air-conditioning, food courts, and larger parking lots, and often they are able to pass those savings along to the consumer.

Attracting quality tenants to its developments is perhaps the most important part of the Mattiace development process. Persuading a major retailer to come to Jackson requires selling not only the development, but the city itself. "We have to let prospective tenants know that Jackson is a growing retail base, that we have the sophisticated, affluent consumers they're looking for," Mattiace says.

"We take great pride in the strong tenant relationships we've developed over the years," Mattiace continues. "We've built a solid reputation for quality site selection and professional execution of the development process, and as a company who can deliver customers to our tenants. We're committed to the success of the individual merchant, as well as to that of the overall center."

AN IMPORTANT JUNCTION

Mattiace Properties' largest undertaking to date has been the Junction Shopping Center at County Line Road and Interstate 55, a busy shopping center anchored by megaretailers Target and Home Depot. Developing the 50-acre site required not only collecting the small parcels that made up the 50 acres, but rerouting a 100-year floodplain and ensuring preservation of Mississippi's Native American heritage.

Adjacent to the busiest commercial corridor in Mississippi, the prime piece of property that became the Junction had previously been dismissed as worthless. A creek meandered through the property, effectively bisecting it. Eighty-nine percent of the tract fell within the 100-year floodplain, rendering this ideally located land unsuitable for development. But Mattiace Properties focused on the property's potential rather than its pitfalls. Mattiace hired the Neel-Schaffer engineering firm to move the creek and design a channel that would contain not only the floodway, but also the 100-year floodplain within the new creek banks.

The next obstacle faced by Mattiace concerned determining whether prehistoric Native American mound sites believed to lie in the area actually existed. A cultural resources survey, archaeological investigation, and excavation were required to prove once and for all that the site was not historically significant.

Finally, the "unusable" property at the southwest corner of I-55 North and County Line Road was ready for development. Today, the Junction includes more than 375,000 square feet of retail space, including the 117,000-square-foot Target store and the 128,000-square-foot Home Depot. Challenges such as those presented by the Junction development are all in a day's work for the company.

"That's what gives retail development its excitement," Mattiace says. "We secure the location, the financing, the contractor, the tenants. We're bringing all of that together to give Jackson-area residents shopping opportunities equal to those found in other major cities." Mattiace Properties, Inc. is helping the state's economic base grow and is enhancing the city's reputation as a great place to live and maintain corporate headquarters.

CLOCKWISE FROM TOP LEFT: MATTIACE PURCHASED AND RESTORED THE LAMAR LIFE BUILDING IN DOWNTOWN JACKSON, A HISTORIC LANDMARK BUILT IN 1927 THAT NOW OFFERS 100,000 SQUARE FEET OF OFFICE SPACE.

ALONG COUNTY LINE ROAD, WHICH IS KNOWN AS THE BUSIEST COMMERCIAL CORRIDOR IN MISSISSIPPI, MATTIACE HAS DEVELOPED SOME 800,000 SQUARE FEET OF RETAIL SPACE.

GROCERY-ANCHORED NEIGHBORHOOD CENTERS ARE AN INTEGAL PART OF THE COMPANY'S LONG-TERM PLAN. PICTURED HERE IS THE SCHOOL STREET CROSSING, WHICH IS ANCHORED BY JITNEY JUNGLE GROCERY.

ADDITIONAL PRINCIPALS AT MATTIACE PROPERTIES INCLUDE (FROM LEFT) JASON MATTIACE, ASSISTANT VICE PRESIDENT; DENIESE THORNHILL, ASSISTANT VICE PRESIDENT; MICHELLE BURFORD, ASSISTANT VICE PRESIDENT, LEASING; AND JERRY VERNON, BROKER

"NOT MANY BUSINESSES DEPEND ON 'RAW MATERIAL' THAT'S WALKING AROUND ON two legs," David Allen, president and CEO of Mississippi Blood Services (MBS), says. "Blood can come only from individuals, and it's up to Mississippi Blood Services to keep a top-of-mind awareness of the need for donors." ✳ The only nonprofit community blood service headquartered in the state, MBS supplies blood to hospitals across Mississippi strictly on a cost-recovery basis.

MBS provides more than half of the blood needed in the state, including the majority of blood required by patients in Jackson.

"Someone in Mississippi needs a pint of blood right now," Allen says. "More than 50 hospitals from the Tennessee border to the Gulf Coast turn to Mississippi Blood Services to provide that blood." In turn, MBS looks to donors to maintain a regular, safe supply, and conducts more than 1,000 blood drives throughout the state every year.

MBS' full-scale blood processing center in Jackson is supported by permanent and mobile donor facilities throughout the state. These collection sites are backed by group-sponsored blood drives held by civic, school, business, and community organizations. All work together to provide a safe, adequate supply of blood, available for patients in any Mississippi hospital.

A Safe, Simple Procedure

Because donated blood cells can be kept for a maximum of 42 days, maintaining an adequate supply is an ongoing challenge. "Our biggest challenge is motivating people to give," Allen says. "We rely totally on voluntarily donated blood, but only 4 to 5 percent of Mississippians donate regularly.

"Some people think that because their blood type is common, they don't need to donate," Allen continues. "Actually, the opposite is true.

The most common blood types are the ones most in demand. The rarest blood type is the one we don't have when we need it."

Almost anyone 17 years old or older and in good health can donate blood every eight weeks. Regular donors have given gallons of their blood over a number of years with absolutely no ill effects to their health. Prospective donors receive a short physical examination prior to donating; if donating could be harmful in any way, the person will not be accepted as a donor.

A normal donation is only one pint of blood, and can be completed in about a half hour. The donor's body reproduces the lost fluid in about 24 hours. Each needle used by MBS is sterile and is used only once. It is not possible to contract AIDS, or any other disease, through donation of blood.

Processing the blood includes typing, testing for certain diseases, screening for antibodies, and other stringent tests—all of which ensure that the blood supply today is safer than it ever has been.

Donated blood is then separated into components, which allows a one-pint donation to benefit several patients. For example, plasma can be used to treat burn victims, platelets could be transfused to a cancer patient undergoing chemotherapy, and red blood cells can be used for surgery, anemia, and dialysis patients. African-American donors play a major role in the fight against sickle-cell anemia. Twenty-five percent of MBS donors are African-American—one of the highest percentages of African-American donors in the nation.

"A single donation can mean life to a child with leukemia, an elderly person facing surgery, or an acci-

A RECENT ADDITION TO THE MISSISSIPPI BLOOD SERVICES FLEET, THE STATE-OF-THE-ART DONOR COACH IS A WELCOME SIGHT AT BLOOD DRIVES FROM THE TENNESSEE BORDER TO THE GULF COAST. COLLECTIVELY, MBS VEHICLES LOG IN 750,000 MILES EACH YEAR FROM MORE THAN 1,000 MOBILE DRIVES AND FROM DAILY DELIVERIES TO NEARLY 60 MISSISSIPPI HOSPITALS.

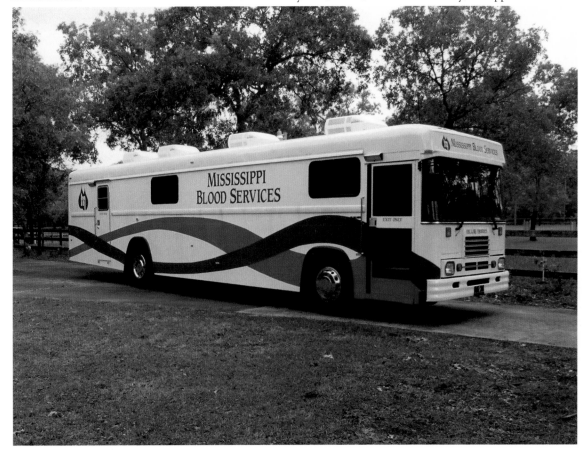

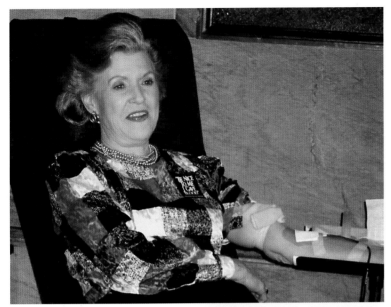

dent victim with internal bleeding," Allen says. "A donor's 30 minutes could give someone else a lifetime." As a way of saying thank-you to its donors, MBS offers donor protection plans that cover all processing fees and blood charges, should the donor require blood for one year from the date of donation. "Blood donors are a special kind of hero," Allen says. "It's not as dramatic as rescuing someone from a burning house, and you may never meet the person you helped, but you're saving a life just the same."

Stewards of the Community Blood Supply

MBS forms partnerships with hospitals that reach beyond the simple distribution of blood products. For example, MBS operates and staffs the transfusion service at the University Medical Center in Jackson, and offers training programs for employees in area hospitals who work with the facility's blood supply.

MBS can provide needed blood to any hospital in Mississippi within three hours. It is the only blood-service organization staffed 24 hours a day, and is also the only blood service in the state with a full-time medical director available to answer hospitals' questions. As a member of Blood Centers of America, a national blood supply consortium, MBS can quickly obtain blood in times of shortage.

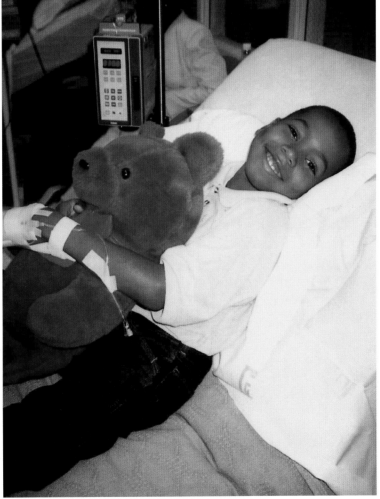

Future plans include developing a North Mississippi operation, adding more drawing-center locations statewide, and continuing to raise awareness of the never-ending need for donors. "People's lives literally depend on how successful we are at performing our job," Allen continues. "Blood is a very precious commodity. MBS is committed to doing everything we can to ensure that it's available, whenever and wherever it's needed."

CLOCKWISE FROM TOP LEFT: MISSISSIPPI FIRST LADY PAT FORDICE GIVES BLOOD AT A JANUARY 1998 BLOOD DRIVE HELD AT THE STATE CAPITOL IN HONOR OF NATIONAL VOLUNTEER BLOOD DONOR MONTH. BEFORE MAKING HER DONATION, FORDICE PRESENTED MBS WITH A PROCLAMATION FROM GOVERNOR KIRK FORDICE, WHICH DESIGNATED JANUARY AS VOLUNTEER BLOOD DONOR MONTH IN MISSISSIPPI.

VOLUNTEERISM IS AN INNATE FAMILY VALUE FOR BROTHERS WESLEY (LEFT) AND CHARLES GANNON. ENTHUSIASTIC PLATELET DONORS, THE GANNONS TO-GETHER HAVE GIVEN MORE THAN 300 TIMES. BEHIND THEM IS A MURAL, DESIGNED EXPRESSLY FOR THE MBS RECEPTION AREA, THAT DEPICTS RE-NOWNED MISSISSIPPIANS, STATE SYMBOLS, AND LANDMARKS.

SICKLE-CELL PATIENT KEITH LAWSON, FROM ROSEDALE, MISSISSIPPI, MUGS FOR THE CAMERA WHILE RECEIVING A BLOOD TRANSFUSION AT THE UNIVERSITY OF MISSISSIPPI MEDICAL CENTER IN JACKSON. ONE IN EVERY SEVEN AFRICAN-AMERICANS IN MISSISSIPPI CARRIES THE SICKLE-CELL TRAIT, AND ONE IN EVERY 400 HAS THIS INCURABLE DISEASE. REGULAR BLOOD TRANSFUSIONS PROVIDE SOME RELIEF FROM THE DISEASE'S PAINFUL SYMPTOMS.

PARKWAY PROPERTIES, INC.

PARKWAY PROPERTIES, INC., A NEW YORK STOCK EXCHANGE-LISTED REAL ESTATE investment trust (REIT) headquartered in Jackson, invests in urban and suburban office buildings in high-growth markets in the southeastern United States and Texas. The company holds the properties for investment purposes, adding to the buildings' value through a hands-on, customer-service-oriented management philosophy. Parkway Realty Services, a wholly owned subsidiary,

provides property management, leasing, and brokerage services to Parkway Properties as well as other third-party owners.

Industry analysts have recognized Parkway as one of the top REITs in the United States; seven of the eight independent financial analysts who follow Parkway have offered it their highest rating. Parkway's shareholders have benefited as well as witnessed a 1,000 percent increase in value since 1992. The secret to the company's success is, first and foremost, superior customer service and an operating philosophy focused on sound investments with disciplined acquisition criteria.

STRICT INVESTMENT CRITERIA

Parkway Properties owns or has interests in more than 48 upscale office buildings encompassing more than 6.5 million square feet of quality office space in 12 states. The company's investment criteria are disciplined, focusing on well-located office buildings ranging from 50,000 to 500,000 square feet. The property must be priced below its current replacement cost.

"Our buying discipline is strict, and we stick to it," says Steve Rogers, president and chief executive officer of Parkway Properties. "We don't believe in growth for growth's sake."

The company invests in markets experiencing significant employment and population growth. "It's important to understand why we are where we are . . . job growth and high employment fill up office buildings," Rogers adds. Parkway's properties are found in Houston, Jackson, Atlanta, Winston-Salem, Dallas, Charlotte, Memphis, Knoxville, Fort Lauderdale, and Little Rock, as well as Columbia, South Carolina, and Richmond, Chesapeake, and northern Virginia. Approximately 25 percent of Parkway's total square footage is located in Houston and 10 percent in Jackson. Parkway's Jackson-owned properties include landmark properties such as One Jackson Place, the Mtel Centre downtown, and the IBM Building on County Line Road/I-55 North.

4-F PROGRAM: CORNERSTONE OF CUSTOMER SERVICE

Parkway's 4-F Program (flags, flowers, fixtures, and fellowship) is the mantra for property enhancements. It is a philosophy of doing the right things at the buildings before being asked to do so. Each of the properties flies both the flag of the United States of America and the appropriate state flag for the location. Fresh flowers are placed throughout the building and rest rooms on a weekly basis, and flowers near the building entrance are rotated seasonally. All landscaping around the buildings and their parking areas is meticulously maintained. Commissioned artwork or exhibits on loan from local museums hang in most lobbies, while outdoor furniture and fixtures enhance exterior common areas. In addition, fellowship is acknowledged to be important. Parkway schedules regular tenant appreciation gatherings, such as breakfasts and lunches, as well as holiday events. Many buildings also offer their tenants free health screenings and other wellness programs.

"We work hard to provide great service for customers in all of our properties," Rogers emphasizes. "We want our customers to enjoy their office space, and we recognize that satisfied tenants are the key to our company's operating success. With high occupancies in our buildings, our biggest risk is that our customers will become unhappy and move out; so all of our actions are oriented toward making it a pleasant experience."

Parkway is committed to the communities in which it invests—especially its hometown, Jackson. Parkway Chairman Leland Speed is the head of its downtown development organization, Capitol Center Inc. Speed states, "Our commitment to our community is evidenced in many ways from landscaping to hiring, involvement, leadership, and caring. We want to help our cities." The officers and employees of Parkway hold numerous leadership roles and board seats in volunteer, church, and community organizations.

When asked what he wants for the future, Rogers replies, "Our goal is simple. We want Parkway Properties to be the best real estate investment trust in America and for our people to be proud to say they work here."

ONE JACKSON PLACE, A CLASS A, 219,000-SQUARE-FOOT BUILDING SITUATED IN THE HEART OF DOWNTOWN, IS THE HOME OF PARKWAY PROPERTIES' CORPORATE OFFICES. THIS BUILDING IS THE SITE OF ALL MAJOR DOWNTOWN EVENTS INCLUDING THE RED BEANS AND RICE FESTIVAL, JUBILEE JAM, AND HOLIDAY JUBILEE.

Horne CPA Group

HORNE CPA GROUP, THE LARGEST INDEPENDENT ACCOUNTING FIRM IN Mississippi, serves clients with operations in more than 20 states. Founded in Laurel in 1962, the company quickly grew from a small hometown firm into an industry leader, whose services extend beyond that of a traditional accounting and consulting firm to servicing industries as diverse as health care, franchises, manufacturers, banks, and construction companies. Now head-

quartered in Jackson, with offices in Mississippi, Tennessee, and Texas, Horne CPA Group ranks among the top 15 accounting firms in the Southeast and among the top 100 firms in the nation.

More Than the Traditional Accounting Firm

When the firm first opened its doors in 1962, its primary clients were local physicians and hospitals, then grappling with financial changes that came as a result of the creation of Medicare. Horne CPA Group assumed a leadership role during the Medicare rollout, establishing support systems and new programs for health care providers, and even assisting the State of Mississippi in developing its first Medicare reimbursement forms.

Over the years, the firm has diversified its areas of concentration beyond accounting, auditing, and financial and tax planning into areas such as employee benefits administration and information technology.

Always a Step Ahead

Horne CPA Group takes the needs of its clients seriously, designing programs and services that help clients keep pace with change and providing educational experiences on specific software programs, tax law changes, and other topics that impact the industries of its clients.

"Our shareholders willingly invest in talent and in technological advances, not simply to meet current demands, but to ensure that this firm is always a step ahead in what we can offer our clients," says Robert R. Ward, CPA and president of Horne CPA Group. Horne CPA Group is focused on two primary goals: To enhance client service by helping its

clients in every field meet the challenges of the new millennium, and to be a prominent force in molding the future of professional accounting services.

Vision for the Future

"We strive to offer services beyond the scope of conventional CPA firms," Ward says. "That means learning as much about our clients' businesses as we can, so that we can offer sound advice—before we're asked for it."

Visionary leadership has been the momentum for the firm's reaching outside the health care industry to meet the demands of clients in other industries. Listening to clients and staying informed about industry trends allow Horne CPA Group professionals to meet the challenges of its clients and provide them with direction for the future.

"OUR MISSION IS TO HELP OUR CLIENTS SUCCEED, WHILE HONORING OUR OBLIGATION TO THE PUBLIC, ALL WITHIN THE FRAMEWORK OF THE STANDARDS OF OUR PROFESSION. WE VALUE OUR CLIENTS, OUR PEOPLE, INNOVATION, LEADERSHIP, TEAMWORK, DOING WHAT'S RIGHT, AND SUCCESS."

RIVER OAKS HEALTH SYSTEM

N 1981, 72 JACKSON-AREA PHYSICIANS FOUNDED A HOSPITAL DIRECTED BY PEOPLE who understood the art of healing and the importance of decisions guided by what was best for the patient. That hospital became River Oaks, a name that has since become synonymous with beyond-the-call health care. ✳ The 221-bed health system is the fifth-largest health care provider in the Jackson area, offering a range of medical services, including outpatient facilities, emergency care, multiple operating rooms, women's health services, a progressive care unit, and a managed care program.

MORE THAN A PATIENT

The River Oaks philosophy is succinctly expressed in the hospital's pledge to patients, which promises, "Before we treat you as a patient, we treat you as a person." Jack Cleary, president and CEO of River Oaks Health System, explains this philosophy: "River Oaks never loses sight of the patient. We strive to get to know each patient as a person, not just as a medical chart. We truly care, and want every patient to experience health care that focuses on compassion and healing."

River Oaks' commitment to patient comfort is reflected in every area of the hospital. Royal Oaks, a special 11-bed unit, provides additional amenities and space for patients and visitors. Private recovery rooms are also available for those in outpatient surgery.

River Oaks' unique Progressive Care Unit treats patients who require continued care after an acute care hospitalization. The Progressive Care Unit offers around-the-clock nursing and individualized services, including physical therapy, speech therapy, cardiopulmonary, dietary, occupational therapy, and social work.

A LEADER IN WOMEN'S HEALTH

River Oaks is a leader in women's health services. In 1994, it opened The Baby Suites, the first labor-delivery-recovery-postpartum (LDRP) obstetrical unit in the Jackson area. Also in 1994, River Oaks acquired Woman's Hospital, renaming the facility River Oaks East-Woman's Pavilion. The Baby Suites at River Oaks and the labor, delivery, and recovery (LDR) rooms at River Oaks East-Woman's Pavilion offer maternity patients and their families a warm, spacious, and comfortable environment in which to welcome a new baby.

EXPANDING SERVICES

River Oaks continually expands its services to better meet the needs of Jackson-area residents. In 1998, River Oaks merged with Health Management Associates, Inc. (HMA), creating a total of more than 30 general acute care hospitals throughout the South. This venture ensures that River Oaks' mission of providing quality care will continue well into the next century.

"The merger is just one more step in our commitment of providing complete care to River Oaks' patients, physicians, and community members," Cleary says. "As our patients will tell you, it's River Oaks' unique blend of care and compassion that sets us apart from other hospitals."

THE PROGRESSIVE CARE UNIT OFFERS AROUND-THE-CLOCK NURSING AND INDIVIDUALIZED SERVICES, INCLUDING PHYSICAL THERAPY, SPEECH THERAPY, CARDIOPULMONARY, DIETARY, OCCUPATIONAL THERAPY, AND SOCIAL WORK (LEFT).

RIVER OAKS IS A LEADER IN WOMEN'S HEALTH SERVICES. ELLEN HILL ENJOYS HER TRIPLETS, WHO WERE BORN AT RIVER OAKS (RIGHT).

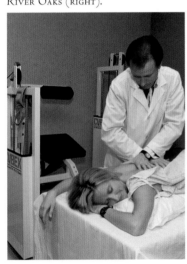

Ask any Jacksonian to name the best place for a business lunch, an anniversary dinner, or a delicious meal, and the overwhelming recommendation is sure to be Nick's. Since 1983, discriminating diners have gathered at the upscale eatery on Lakeland Drive to partake of the discreet service, intimate atmosphere, and what is arguably the best cuisine in Jackson. ✳ "We stress consistency," Owner and Head Chef Nick Apostle says. "Consistency in food, atmosphere, and service. If a restaurant is not going to be consistent, it's not going to be a restaurant long."

ALWAYS A DELIGHTFUL EXPERIENCE

On any given day, some 375 diners enjoy lunch or dinner at Nick's, sampling the city's finest seafood, beef, pork, and poultry. While the entrées are generous, regular patrons know to save room for one of the restaurant's many tempting desserts, and to bring along a companion willing to split a tasty appetizer or two.

The spacious dining room at Nick's is complemented by a cozy, comfortable lounge, ideal for relaxing with a glass of wine before dinner, socializing with friends after hours, or discussing the latest business happenings. The tranquil atmosphere is complemented by one of Jackson's finest wine lists.

Service at Nick's is nothing short of impeccable. Staff members display a unique mix of formality and southern hospitality, and some know the regulars by name and by cocktail preference. Local polls invariably point to the wait staff at Nick's as the best in town.

To rank Nick's among the best restaurants not only in Mississippi, but in the entire South is no exaggeration. Nick Apostle was the only chef in Jackson, and one of only three in Mississippi, selected as one of the Discovery Channel's Great Chefs of the South.

THE "NICK" BEHIND NICK'S

Nick Apostle began his career in the restaurant business at the tender age of 12. His father, Paul Apostle, owned a chain of restaurants, and was more than happy to introduce his son to every level of the business, from dish washing to food preparation. Following college graduation, a 10-year stint managing one of his father's restaurants, and courses at the Culinary Institute in Hyde Park, New York, Nick Apostle returned to Jackson to fulfill his dream of operating a premier, white tablecloth restaurant.

Things got off to a rocky start. Two weeks after Nick's celebrated its grand opening, the head chef quit. Apostle donned an apron and took over, filling the role of chef for the next 14 years. In the early days, business was slow, and Nick's survived largely due to the steadfast support of a handful of regulars, whose names now adorn brass plaques next to their usual booths.

The turning point came two months after the restaurant's opening, when the *Jackson Clarion-Ledger* published a four-star review. The following day, crowds had lined up by lunchtime, and business hasn't slowed down since.

In 1997, Apostle hired an executive chef so he could spend more time in the dining room, greeting his loyal patrons—who include local politicians, best-selling authors, and Hollywood actors—and meeting new customers.

"My goal is to make Nick's a Jackson institution, and again, that all comes down to consistency of product and service," Apostle says. "I want people to know they can bring their family, business associates, or special guests here and have a good experience every time."

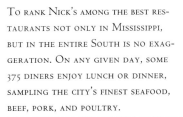

To rank Nick's among the best restaurants not only in Mississippi, but in the entire South is no exaggeration. On any given day, some 375 diners enjoy lunch or dinner, sampling the city's finest seafood, beef, pork, and poultry.

CommuniGroup

WITH THE DIVESTITURE OF AT&T IN 1982, COMMUNIGROUP BECAME THE first alternative long-distance carrier to service Mississippi. The company began offering long-distance service to business customers in Jackson, running the entire operation with just three employees. Today, CommuniGroup provides long-distance service to hundreds of thousands of business and residential customers throughout the southeastern United

States. The company markets long-distance services in Alabama, Arkansas, Louisiana, Mississippi, and Tennessee, with corporate headquarters in downtown Jackson. CommuniGroup is a subsidiary of Telephone Electronics Corporation (TEC), the largest privately held telecommunications company in the country.

COMMUNICATIONS MADE EASY

CommuniGroup attributes its success to a simple philosophy: communications made easy. "CommuniGroup is a customer-focused company. Unlike some of the larger long-distance companies, we're willing to adapt to a customer's individual needs," says Robert F. Chafin, CommuniGroup's president.

"We provide quick decisions and fast responses, all in an effort to make our customers' lives easier," says Chafin. "Like our customers, CommuniGroup is convenience oriented, cost conscious, and progressive. Every CommuniGroup product or service is designed to be easy to use and easy on the pocketbook."

The company's products and services include 1+ dialing, cellular 1+ dialing, 800 and 888 numbers, 800 access calling cards, 800 access conference calling, custom calling plans, and private line services.

CommuniGroup measures its success not only by the growth of its customer base, but also by customer reaction to new products. The company's entrepreneurial spirit is reflected in many services offered only by CommuniGroup. For example, CommuniGroup's Conference on Demand is a one-of-a-kind service that connects up to 20 participants at once without assistance from an operator. Conferencing access using the Connect-Card makes conference calling easy for customers on the road. And CommuniGroup has recently introduced the sale of prepaid long-distance cards through regional ATMs.

For sports enthusiasts, the company's Game Pass service allows fans to listen to university football game broadcasts via any telephone in the United States. CommuniGroup has also created specialized products to help nonprofit organizations in raising funds. Long-distance calling clubs allow participants to donate money to particular groups on a monthly basis as part of their normal long-distance calling. CommuniGroup's future plans include building on the company's arsenal of long-distance services, and expanding into new areas, including Internet and local telephone service opportunities.

A COMMUNITY LEADER

CommuniGroup has long been a supporter of civic and cultural events in Jackson, and frequently donates its unique services to meet needs in the community. During the Christmas season, CommuniGroup provides free long-distance calling cards to families of patients in the Children's Hospital at the University of Mississippi Medical Center. Through its Lineman of the Year program, CommuniGroup makes donations to Mississippi universities in honor of outstanding student athletes. CommuniGroup also provides support to Jackson's Power Academic and Performing Arts Complex (APAC) program by recognizing talented high school seniors and their accomplishments.

In the professional arena, Chafin has been a member of the Mississippi Telecommunications Task Force, formed to address issues facing the state's burgeoning telecommunications industry and to create new opportunities for telecommunications firms. "Jackson is growing rapidly in the telecommunications area," Chafin says, "and CommuniGroup is proud to be a part of that success story."

HUBERT WORLEY JR.

FRIEDE GOLDMAN INTERNATIONAL INC.

FRIEDE GOLDMAN INTERNATIONAL INC. IS THE ONLY COMPANY IN THE world that offers a full range of design and construction services for the offshore drilling industry, including offshore vessel design and engineering, repair and retrofitting, new-build construction, equipment, and financing. The company, which is headquartered in Jackson, holds 34 percent of the worldwide market for semisubmersible offshore drilling designs, which are floating oil rigs capable of

drilling in waters as deep as 10,000 feet. These vessels are found in the Gulf of Mexico, Europe, Canada, South America, China, Asia, West Africa, and the North Sea. Friede Goldman also claims more than 10 percent of the market for jack-up rigs, which are attached to the ocean floor.

CHRIS SALVO

THE INDUSTRY PIONEER
Friede Goldman International is the parent company of HAM Marine, Inc., a Pascagoula-based company specializing in offshore rig modification and retrofits. HAM Marine has 16 years' experience in the repair, retrofit, and conversion of offshore drilling rigs—more than any other shipyard in the Gulf of Mexico.

Another subsidiary of Friede Goldman International Inc. (FGII) is Friede & Goldman, Ltd. (F&G), a naval architectural and marine engineering and design firm based in New Orleans. The world's leading independent designer of mobile offshore drilling vessels, Friede & Goldman, Ltd. has created pioneering designs since 1947. F&G founder Jerome L. Goldman is known in the industry as the Dean of the Drill Rig Architects.

STATE-OF-THE-ART FACILITIES IN THE UNITED STATES AND CANADA
The company owns two shipyards in Pascagoula, including a new yard opened in 1998. Friede Goldman Offshore, a state-of-the-art manufacturing facility, is the most modern shipyard built in North America in the last 30 years. In 1997, Friede Goldman acquired two Canadian shipyards in order to gain greater access to the North Sea and European markets. These two year-round

CHRIS SALVO

manufacturing and repair facilities comprise Friede Goldman Newfoundland, the largest fabricator in Newfoundland. Friede Goldman purchased the pair, estimated to be worth $100 million, from the Canadian government for $1 and labor guarantees. Employing more than 2,500 at its shipyards and subsidiaries, Friede Goldman has a growing sales and marketing office in Houston, where many of its customers are located.

SOARING STOCK AND CONTINUED INVESTMENT
Friede Goldman International Inc. went public in 1997 in one of the most successful initial public offerings (IPO) of the year. A report from Bear, Stearns, and Co. highly recommended investing in the company, stating, "Friede Goldman . . . represents a compelling opportunity for investors to capitalize on the rising demand for offshore drilling rigs."

"Our successful IPO shows the level of confidence placed in us to continue to operate in a profitable, well-organized manner," J.L. Holloway, Friede Goldman International chairman and CEO, says. Friede Goldman continues to invest heavily in the research and development of new offshore drilling vessel designs, and keeps an eye out for acquisitions that will enhance its physical and technical capabilities. For example, FGII's acquisition of France Marine and its subsidiaries in February 1998 gave the company the ability to manufacture critical components used in building offshore drilling units, while expanding its product lines and worldwide operations base. Headquartered in Nantes, France, the companies are global leaders in the design and manufacture of marine and offshore equipment.

"Friede Goldman has built a reputation on making smart moves at the right time, then following through with good management and a highly skilled, productive workforce," Holloway says. "Our goal is to be the world's premier offshore oil services company."

HAM MARINE, INC., FOUNDED IN 1982 IN PASCAGOULA, MISSISSIPPI, BECAME THE CORNERSTONE OF FRIEDE GOLDMAN INTERNATIONAL, A LEADER IN THE OFFSHORE OIL SERVICES INDUSTRY.

WorldCom

JN November 1997, Jackson-based WorldCom, Inc. and MCI Communications Corp. proposed the largest corporate merger in U.S. history. The $37 billion purchase of MCI by WorldCom would make the new company the second-largest long-distance telephone company in the United States. Jackson has become home to one of the largest communications companies in the world, and Bernie Ebbers—the colorful president and CEO of WorldCom who masterminded

the acquisition—has become a household name in Jackson.

From Humble Beginnings to Unprecedented Growth
In 1983, Ebbers, a former milkman and junior high school coach, joined three other investors in starting a long-distance resale company. One of the early planning meetings was held in a restaurant where a waitress is credited with naming the company by scribbling

"Long Distance Discount Calling" (later changed to Long Distance Discount Service, or LDDS) on a napkin.

LDDS provided its first minute of long-distance service to the University of Southern Mississippi in 1984. For most of the first year of operation, the company's board met in the Western Sizzler in Hattiesburg. Ebbers, who was previously only a passive investor, was recruited to take over as CEO in 1985 because the company had been operating in the red since its inception. According to an early investor, "The only experience Bernie had in operating a long-distance company was that he had used the phone." Apparently, that was all the experience Ebbers needed. Under his leadership, the company's stock appreciated an average of 57 percent per year, thereby placing the company at the top of the *Wall Street Journal*'s 1996 Shareholder Scoreboard for return to shareholders over a 10-year period.

Through a series of well-planned mergers and acquisitions, LDDS quickly expanded its service area to include the entire United States and more than 200 foreign countries. In 1995, LDDS changed its name to WorldCom, reflecting its global aspirations in the communications industry. In the five years prior to the proposed MCI merger, WorldCom acquired or merged with more than 40 companies. Motivated sales teams met targets that many thought impossible, and by the time the MCI deal was announced, WorldCom had grown to become the nation's fourth-largest long-distance provider.

Growing the Distance
WorldCom serves 6 percent of the long-distance market with 1 million business customers (pre-merger). With 200 offices worldwide, WorldCom is a large carrier of international voice traffic.

The proposed MCI merger came on the heels of WorldCom's September 1997 acquisition of the Internet service provider CompuServe and the competitive local telecommunication services provider Brooks Fiber. WorldCom is one of the nation's leading Internet service providers.

A company that began as an idea in a coffee shop and grew to become one of the world's largest communications companies in the span of 14 years, WorldCom has succeeded in the competitive long-distance marketplace by growing constantly to meet consumers' needs. Throughout its evolution, the company has always striven to provide customers with the best telephone service that modern technology can offer. In the future, WorldCom will continue to expand its offerings as advances in communications technology bring new ways for people to exchange ideas and information in the 21st century.

Clockwise from top:
The six-story building on Amite Street in downtown Jackson has served as corporate headquarters for WorldCom since 1993. To accommodate its burgeoning workforce, the company took on two additional Jackson sites.

A new, 550,000-square-foot corporate headquarters facility was constructed in Clinton, just west of Jackson, in 1997-1998 and is expected to house approximately 2,000 employees.

WorldCom's Jackson Data Center will occupy a more expansive, state-of-the-art facility when it moves to its new, 12,000-square-foot home at the Clinton site.

NORTHPARK MALL

I N THE EARLY 1980S, THE EASTERN END OF COUNTY LINE ROAD WAS LITTLE MORE than an empty field. Then came Cadillac-Fairview, a savvy retail development company based in Toronto. Noting that population growth in the Jackson metro area was focused on northeast Jackson and the nearby communities of Ridgeland and Madison, Cadillac-Fairview suspected the area was ripe for retail development, and began work on plans for an upscale mall. Today, the County Line Road corridor is a

shopping mecca, anchored by Cadillac-Fairview's retail masterpiece, Northpark Mall.

A SHOPPER'S PARADISE

Northpark is Mississippi's premier shopping destination, attracting sophisticated shoppers and just-for-fun browsers from a 100-mile radius. The mall is home to more than 125 specialty shops, department stores, and restaurants, many of which are found nowhere else in Mississippi, such as Abercrombie & Fitch, Banana Republic, Ann Taylor, Warner Brothers Studio Store, Brookstone, Eddie Bauer, and Caché.

The mall is also home to Williams-Sonoma, Disney Store, The Nature Company, The Limited, Godiva Chocolatiers, Bath and Body Works, Victoria's Secret, Body Shop, Nine West, and dozens of other upscale retailers. Anchor tenants include Dillard's, Gayfers, J.C. Penney, and McRae's department stores.

Boasting a 97 percent occupancy rate, Northpark is home to more shops than any other mall in Jackson, and annual sales surpass the $100 million mark. "Northpark is the cutting edge of retail in Mississippi," says Susan Marquez, marketing director. "Offering a variety of shops and restaurants is very important to maintaining that edge. We constantly analyze our tenant mix to be sure we're giving our customers the merchandise they're looking for. We strive to give our customers a unique shopping experience."

MORE THAN MERCHANDISE

Reaching beyond retail sales, Northpark impacts the community by sponsoring recreational and cultural events in the Jackson area, such as the annual Jubilee! JAM music festival and the Sky Parade air show. Northpark's signature event is the annual Balloon Glow, held in partnership with the Mississippi Championship Hot Air

Balloon Festival, the City of Ridgeland, and the Ridgeland Tourism Board. Some 40 hot air balloons fill a field adjacent to the mall, creating a visual delight that attracts more than 60,000 spectators. "Our contribution to the Jackson area doesn't begin or end at the mall entrance," Marquez says. "Northpark is proud to be an active part of the metro Jackson community."

NORTHPARK MALL IS HOME TO MORE THAN 125 SPECIALTY SHOPS, DEPARTMENT STORES, AND RESTAURANTS, ATTRACTING SHOPPERS FROM A 100-MILE RADIUS (TOP).

IN THE EARLY 1980S, THE EASTERN END OF COUNTY LINE ROAD WAS LITTLE MORE THAN AN EMPTY FIELD. TODAY, THE COUNTY LINE ROAD CORRIDOR IS A SHOPPING MECCA, ANCHORED BY CADILLAC-FAIRVIEW'S NORTHPARK MALL (BOTTOM).

LTM Enterprises, Inc./McDonald's

In 1984, LeRoy Walker had two goals: to own his own business and to have a positive influence on young people. The former schoolteacher accomplished both objectives by becoming a McDonald's restaurant operator. "I felt I could give more to the community as a franchisee than as a teacher," says Walker, president and owner of LTM Enterprises, Inc., a 10-restaurant franchise in Jackson. * "I saw the role McDonald's plays in society as an employer of youth," Walker says. "McDonald's gives back to the community by giving teenagers their first jobs. As a McDonald's franchisee, I have more resources and can directly create more opportunities for young people."

From Classroom to Fast Food

Walker joined the McDonald's team in 1984, when he acquired a McDonald's restaurant in Omaha, Nebraska, thus ending a 12-year career as a high school teacher. Five years later, he sold his Omaha franchise and purchased five units in Jackson. He has since built three new McDonald's restaurants and acquired two existing ones in Jackson. Collectively, Walker's restaurants generate some $10.5 million in total annual sales.

While Walker is proud of his business accomplishments, providing opportunities and inspiration for young employees is still LTM Enterprise's primary focus. "It is critical for our employees to understand that it doesn't matter if you own one restaurant or 50 restaurants," Walker says. "They must see that you have to work hard to achieve your goals."

Inspiration for Youth and for Jackson

High school students who work in Walker's restaurants must show him their grades each quarter. Students whose grades suffer because of their workload are furloughed until they show improvement.

In addition to monitoring the progress of his own employees, Walker flexes the financial strength of his franchise, backing local school programs and youth-oriented community projects. LTM Enterprises sponsors an annual speech and essay contest in honor of Dr. Martin Luther King Jr.,

awarding more than $3,000 in cash prizes to students in the Jackson Public Schools system.

Walker has become one of Jackson's most active and respected business leaders, and one of the most civic-minded operators in the McDonald's system. He was inducted into the Mississippi Business Hall of Fame in 1995, and was elected chairman of the Greater Jackson Chamber of Commerce in 1998. LTM Enterprises was named the 1993 Minority Retail Firm of the Year by the Minority Business Development Agency of the U.S. Chamber of Commerce.

Award-Winning Success

Walker's efforts have also earned numerous accolades from McDonald's corporate offices. He has received both the Golden Arch Operator of the Year Award and the Mac TLC Award for Outstanding Community Service.

"I've gotten as much out of being a McDonald's operator as I've put into it," Walker says. "The restaurants have provided me with the resources I needed to make a difference, and McDonald's has given me the autonomy to make decisions that are in the best interest of the community."

HORRELL PHOTOGRAPHY

"McDonald's gives back to the community by giving teenagers their first jobs," says LeRoy Walker, founder of LTM Enterprises, Inc. "As a McDonald's franchisee, I have more resources and can directly create more opportunities for young people."

HARRIS CONSTRUCTORS, INC.

BEGINNING WITH A MERE FOUR EMPLOYEES IN 1989, HARRIS Constructors, Inc. has grown to include more than 50 employees and utilizes hundreds of subcontractors. Originally providing general construction and construction management services for clients primarily in central Mississippi, the company has expanded its market area to include projects in Louisiana, Kentucky, North Carolina, South Carolina,

and West Virginia. "Our goal isn't to be the largest construction company in Mississippi, but to provide construction of the highest quality," says David Harris, founder and owner of Harris Constructors.

STRINGENT QUALITY CONTROL

In spite of its steady growth, Harris Constructors remains committed to a stringent level of quality control and an attention to detail that sets the company apart from its competition. "We take on a limited number of projects, which allows us to give each job the attention it deserves," Harris says. "Because we never overcommit our resources and we purposely control our growth, we're able to guarantee the highest level of quality in our construction."

LOCAL AND INTERNATIONAL PROJECTS

Harris Constructors' work is represented in office buildings, shopping centers, banks, churches, and manufacturing plants. Recent projects in the Jackson area include the Centre Park North/Irby Lighting Center in Ridgeland, Ridgecrest Baptist Church and Liberty Park in Madison, Paine Webber/IBM building in Jackson, St. Marks Methodist Church in Brandon, renovation of Ayer Hall at Jackson State University, Methodist Hospital's Community Medical Centers, and a number of Jitney Jungle grocery stores.

In addition to local projects, Harris Constructors reaches into the international realm. A memorable job far from Mississippi was the construction of a Nexrad radar installation in Portugal for the Lockheed Martin company. The project was located at the Lajes air force base on the island of Terceira in the Azores island chain.

OLD-TIME RELIGION AND MODERN TECHNOLOGY

While Harris Constructors handles a variety of projects, church building and communications-related construction have become the firm's specialties. "We've probably built more churches in the central Mississippi area than any other contractor," Harris says. "The people who serve on the church building committees are usually straightforward, honest people with whom we enjoy working. By helping local churches build facilities, we're helping to build the Kingdom."

Harris Constructors is also recognized for its expertise in communications-related construction. Communications leaders—including BellSouth, BellSouth Mobility, and AT&T—rely on Harris to build and renovate communication towers, office space, and equipment switching centers, as well as other highly specialized projects.

BUILDING THE COMMUNITY AND THE INDUSTRY

Harris Constructors is a leader in the community as well as in the construction industry. The company holds membership in the Ridgeland Chamber of Commerce, and Harris is a member of the chamber's board of directors. He was a longtime board member and president of the Madison-Ridgeland Youth Club, which organized recreational sports teams for more than 1,500 children in southern Madison County. On an industry level, Harris has served as a director for the Associated General Contractors of Mississippi and as chairman of the Mississippi Construction Foundation.

As his company continues to grow, Harris stands by his original business philosophy: "We'll continue to give our clients the individual attention they deserve, and continue to build projects of which our company and our clients can be proud."

RECENT HARRIS CONSTRUCTORS PROJECTS IN THE JACKSON AREA INCLUDE THE CENTRE PARK NORTH/IRBY LIGHTING CENTER IN RIDGELAND (LEFT) AND RIDGECREST BAPTIST CHURCH.

LEXTRON CORPORATION

LEXTRON CORPORATION, A SMALL MANUFACTURER OF ELECTRICAL AND ELECTRONIC assemblies for the telecommunications and automotive industries, is the brainchild of Charles Doty, company president. ✳ Raised and educated in a poverty-stricken region of the Mississippi Delta, Doty had long harbored the dream of establishing and operating his own electronics firm. Eight years after receiving his MBA from Jackson State University, Doty had built a successful career working for other companies, but continued to spend every spare moment planning and developing the idea for his own small business. In 1991, Doty's dream was realized when Lextron Corporation opened for business in the Jackson Enterprise Center, a small-business incubator.

PROVING THAT BIGGER ISN'T ALWAYS BETTER

Lextron's biggest challenge was proving that a small company—at that time, having fewer than 10 employees—could deliver the superior product needed to succeed in the highly competitive electronics industry. The opportunity came in 1993, when BellSouth awarded Lextron its first major piece of business: a contract to assemble electronic cable wire harnesses. Lextron proved that a small company could provide superior quality performance, completing the project with a zero-defect rate.

BellSouth was so pleased with the company's work that it featured Lextron in a video presentation highlighting successful minority-owned businesses.

In 1995, AT&T awarded Lextron a major contract to manufacture devices that protect telephone lines from inclement weather and high-voltage surges. The contract increased Lextron's number of employees from 10 to 25. In 1996, a growing Lextron acquired additional space at the Jackson Enterprise Center.

By the end of 1997, the company had been awarded another major contract, this time by the Delphi Packard Electric Systems Division of General Motors; had acquired its own, 50,000-square-foot facility; and employed nearly 100 workers.

A SMALL-BUSINESS SUCCESS STORY

In 1996, Lextron received the prestigious Governor's Cup Award, presented by the Southern Growth Policies Board in recognition of outstanding efforts in economic development. Criteria include economic impact of the company on its community relative to its size, community involvement by the company and its employees, and the company's involvement in developing its human resources. Lextron was nominated for the award by the Mississippi Governor's Office, and was chosen the winner in the small-business category from among 14 businesses nominated from 14 southeastern states.

Doty has received numerous awards for his outstanding business leadership, including the Entrepreneur of the Year award presented by the Forward Lookers Federated Club, an organization dedicated to improving social, moral, religious, and educational levels in Mississippi. He also has been recognized in the *Mississippi Business Journal*'s Top 40 Under 40 program.

SURVIVAL IN THE HIGHLY COMPETITIVE ELECTRONICS INDUSTRY HAS REQUIRED LEXTRON TO PROVE THAT A SMALL COMPANY CAN DELIVER A SUPERIOR PRODUCT.

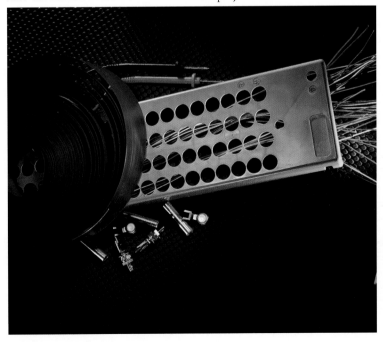

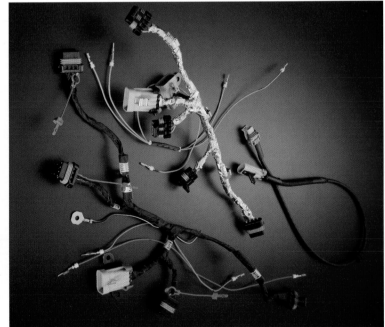

Doty is a member of the State of Mississippi's Telecommunications Task Force, formed to expand opportunities for the state's growing telecommunications industry.

Doty is also involved in a number of civic and charitable concerns, serving as a member of the *Clarion-Ledger*'s Reader Editorial Board and on the boards of Habitat for Humanity, American Heart Association, and Friends of Educational Television. Following the lead of its founder, Lextron is a civic-minded company, committed to reinvesting in the community through organizations such as Habitat for Humanity.

The backbone of Lextron's operations is the assembly line workers, most of whom are women and many of whom are single mothers from the Jackson area. "I appreciate the commitment and dedication these workers have made to the growth of Lextron. Because of this, I want to create a quality day care center: one that is more than a baby-sitter, and also has a good learning component," Doty says. National attention has already been drawn to the problem of quality day care, and many businesses are seeing the benefits of providing this service. Lextron hopes its efforts will encourage businesses in the Jackson area to join national trends. As an incentive to give people pride in their work, Lextron is currently developing a profit-sharing plan for its employees. As further evidence of Lextron's priority on the workforce, it has organized the plants to work a four-day week, giving employees a three-day weekend. "I find that my employees, especially the mothers, value a weekday off so they can visit schools and see how their children are doing," states Doty.

A recent article in the *Mississippi Business Journal* praised both Lextron's success and Doty's personal and professional achievements: "When people mention the name of Charles Doty, it's a given that the reference will be respectful of his business achievements and philosophy."

FOUNDED IN 1994, MISSISSIPPI MANAGED CARE NETWORK, INC. (MMCN) was one of Mississippi's first statewide health maintenance organizations (HMOs). MMCN administers the Access . . . Plan, a managed care system that provides enrollees with cost-effective health care services and wellness programs. Jesse A. Buie, MMCN's founder and president, created the HMO and the Access . . . Plan with the help and input of health care professionals nationwide.

MISSISSIPPI MANAGED CARE NETWORK, INC. (MMCN) SPONSORS THE GOOD SHOTS SAVES LIVES IMMUNIZATION PROGRAM, WHICH REWARDS PARENTS WHO KEEP THEIR CHILDREN'S IMMUNIZATIONS UP TO DATE WITH FREE CHILD CARE PRODUCTS.

Buie explains, "Mississippi Managed Care was founded with a twofold mission: to provide quality, affordable health care that is accessible to everyone and to design a system that would adequately compensate doctors and other health care professionals." MMCN has been successful on both counts.

THE MEDICAID MANAGED CARE PILOT PROGRAM

MMCN was one of four HMOs originally chosen to participate in the Mississippi Medicaid Managed Care Pilot Program, initially offered in Forrest, Hancock, Harrison, Lauderdale, Warren, and Washington counties. Under the pilot program, Medicaid recipients are given a choice of continuing traditional Medicaid coverage or enrolling with one of the participating HMOs. The state pays MMCN a premium for each participant who enrolls. MMCN then manages the complete health care of that participant.

The premium the state pays MMCN is 10 percent less than the state was paying previously. According to Buie, MMCN offers a higher quality and quantity of services at a lower cost than the traditional Medicaid system. "Medicaid is a program established to pay bills, not to manage health care," Buie says. "It's up to HMOs and health care providers to actively manage health care and to find the most cost-effective way to do it."

Participants who select MMCN receive immediate benefits over traditional Medicaid coverage. For example, Medicaid recipients are limited to five prescriptions per month. MMCN does not place a limit on prescriptions, believing patients should have access to as many medications as are necessary to keep them healthy. And when the state eliminated HIV drug benefits for Medicaid patients, MMCN continued to cover its enrollees' HIV medications. "We are a compassionate company," Buie says. "When we promise our participants 'a quality health plan your family can trust,' it's more than just a catchy slogan."

Enrollees also have access to more than 300 top physicians in the MMCN provider network, many of whom do not normally treat Medicaid patients. MMCN simplifies the compensation process for participating providers and pays these physicians more than they would receive from Medicaid. "We encourage physicians to take a certain percentage of the Medicaid population," Buie says. "We pay our providers on time, we pay them more than they were receiving from Medicaid before MMCN, and the patients receive better care in a more coordinated fashion. It's a win-win situation."

THE COMMERCIAL PROGRAM

MMCN's next step has been the launch of its commercial plans that will allow MMCN to manage employee health care for Mississippi companies,

▲ GREG CAMPBELL PHOTOGRAPHY

serving groups as small as two members. The MMCN plans reach beyond the benefits provided by traditional health insurance. MMCN not only pays claims, but contracts with health care providers for services. Employers receive comprehensive coverage for their employees at a competitive price, including wellness benefits, such as regular checkups, baby care, immunizations, and other advantages not covered by traditional health insurance. MMCN's commercial plans, based on the company's success in the public sector, give employers practical and desirable solutions to the problem of rising health care costs. An ever increasing number of employers are starting to recognize the potential of the managed care solution. With its history of service, focus on prevention, and affordability for both employers and employees, Mississippi Managed Care Network, Inc. is ready to fill the current need and to adapt to future changes in the health care industry.

Promoting Wellness

"One of the most important things we do is make preventive health care services affordable," Buie says. "Helping people stay well instead of waiting to treat them when they're sick is the key to providing economical health care." Toward that goal, MMCN sponsors a variety of programs promoting healthy lifestyles. Managed care with MMCN encompasses many facets, including preventive care and wellness benefits. The Good Shots Saves Lives campaign and essay contest invites children to write compositions stressing the importance of immunizations; winners receive a trip to a professional basketball game. In addition, the Good Shots Saves Lives immunization program rewards parents who keep their children's immunizations up to date with free child care products. Managed care also includes the Mom-2-Be Club, an educational and wellness benefit for pregnant women of all ages that stresses the importance of prenatal care. Club members receive a coupon book redeemable for gifts each time they visit a doctor as part of a prenatal care program. MMCN also spon-

sors a statewide calendar art contest that is used by schools and teachers as a springboard for health and safety lessons.

Other MMCN outreach programs include community health fairs that offer preventive health education, health screening, and early detection of possible health problems. MMCN's educational efforts aim at heightening awareness about nutrition, disease prevention, and many other health care concerns.

Such efforts creatively approach people and communities that have historically lacked the opportunity

ENROLLEES HAVE ACCESS TO MORE THAN 300 TOP PHYSICIANS IN THE MMCN PROVIDER NETWORK (TOP).

THE MOM-2-BE CLUB IS AN EDUCATIONAL AND WELLNESS BENEFIT PROGRAM FOR PREGNANT WOMEN OF ALL AGES THAT STRESSES THE IMPORTANCE OF PRENATAL CARE. CLUB MEMBERS RECEIVE A COUPON BOOK REDEEMABLE FOR GIFTS EACH TIME THEY VISIT A DOCTOR AS PART OF A PRENATAL CARE PROGRAM (BOTTOM).

for comprehensive health care. Through its emphasis on preventive care of all kinds, Mississippi Managed Care Network, Inc. treats health problems when they are most treatable—in their early stages. "Wellness care and preventive measures can radically reduce many of the major health and medical problems facing Mississippi, including high blood pressure, strokes, teen pregnancy, and infant mortality," Buie stresses. "The whole health care system benefits from keeping the population well, and it's up to HMOs like Mississippi Managed Care Network, Inc. to make it happen."

UNION PLANTERS BANK

UNION PLANTERS BANK ESTABLISHED ITSELF IN THE JACKSON MARKET IN 1994 WITH the acquisition of Mississippi-based Sunburst Bank. Today, Union Planters' Jackson-based region operates locations in 20 central Mississippi communities, carrying on a legacy of local involvement in cities and towns across the state. ✳ Union Planters offices are strategically located across the city of Jackson and in Jackson Metro communities including Madison, Ridgeland, Pearl, Brandon,

UNION PLANTERS' MAIN OFFICE ON CAPITOL STREET IN THE HEART OF DOWNTOWN JACKSON IS A PHYSICAL REMINDER OF THE BANK'S INVOLVEMENT IN THE COMMUNITY. A JACKSON LANDMARK IN ITSELF, THE BUILDING IS WIDELY CONSIDERED TO BE ONE OF THE REGION'S FINEST EXAMPLES OF NEOCLASSIC ARCHITECTURE.

Byram, and Clinton. Retail and commercial customers take advantage of a variety of traditional products, as well as specialized financial services such as alternative investments, commercial and residential real estate, cash management services, and trust and investment management. This banking network also encompasses three segment-focused business

lines—CorporateBanc, BusinessBanc, and PrivateBanc—dedicated to serving the needs of the city's large commercial customers, small businesses, and professionals. The Union Planters philosophy lies in a one-on-one approach: a banker and a customer working together to find the best solution to that customer's need, no matter how simple or sophisticated.

A VISIBLE CIVIC LEADER

Built in 1905, Union Planters' main office on Capitol Street in the heart of downtown Jackson is a physical reminder of the bank's involvement in the community. A Jackson landmark in itself, the building is widely considered to be one of the region's finest examples of neoclassic architecture.

Union Planters is also visible through its participation in a number of economic, civic, social, and cultural activities across the capital city. The bank is a strong supporter of the Mississippi Symphony Orchestra, International Ballet Competition, Mississippi Museum of Art, and New Stage Theatre, as well as Habitat for Humanity, numerous Adopt-A-School programs, and United Way of the Capital Area. In addition, Union Planters donated the Alamo Theatre, a local African-American landmark, to the Farish Street District, an African-American heritage and cultural center.

With a proud and colorful heritage, and a tradition of community service that only continues to grow, Union Planters Bank has much to be proud of in Jackson. According to Jack Garner, president and CEO, "Union Planters' crowning achievement is pleasing our customers. Nothing is more valuable than a satisfied customer who refers others to Union Planters."

Union Planters Corporation is headquartered in Memphis and was founded in 1869. In 1987, Union Planters began acquiring other banks, and by 1998, had become an $18 billion bank holding company with banking offices in eight states, including Mississippi, Tennessee, Arkansas, Louisiana, Alabama, Missouri, Florida, and Kentucky.

GIL FORD PHOTOGRAPHY

ValuePage is built around our customers' needs and desire for wireless coverage and service," says Wirt Yerger III, president of ValuePage. "We provide complete coverage in our market areas where our customers need it, and we're priced competitively. Those are the basic pluses that keep us where we want to be: a good product at a good price." * Through a series of acquisitions and internal growth, ValuePage developed from a simple paging provider into an

integrated product mix that now includes one- and two-way paging, voice mail, E-mail, and cellular telephone service. "Our product mix has made us profitable in an industry in which many companies are not," Yerger says. "Customers in Mississippi, Alabama, and Florida turn to ValuePage for one-stop shopping for their wireless communications needs."

ValuePage is a carrier as well as a major reseller for dominant paging companies throughout the Southeast, and it is also one of the larger agents for BellSouth Mobility and Cellular South in Mississippi. ValuePage offers excellent coverage, state-of-the-art equipment, and total service and technical support in both the paging and cellular arenas. Through agreements with multiple paging and cellular carriers, the company offers competitively priced, customized paging and cellular coverage. ValuePage retail stores can be found in Jackson and McComb, Mississippi; Tuscaloosa, Mobile, and Daphne, Alabama; and Pensacola, Florida.

The largest privately held paging company in the state, ValuePage is owned primarily by Mississippians. Yerger was working for his family's Mississippi insurance firm, Jackson-based Ross & Yerger, when he began investing in wireless communications. Eventually, Yerger decided to leave the insurance field and go into the telecommunications business full-time.

In 1994, Yerger and several investors purchased the paging assets of AnswerStat, a Jackson-based answering service. The new company, named ValuePage, then expanded

its business through internal growth and with the purchases of Tuscaloosa-based PageLink and CellPage in McComb.

In late 1995, ValuePage then merged with another local company, TelComm South. TelComm had long been a BellSouth Mobility (then MCTA) cellular agent and was named Outstanding Agent of the Year for five consecutive years. ValuePage is building on the successful business alliance.

Yerger emphasizes that it is the customer who has the most to gain from the dizzying array of competition common to the telecommunications industry. "Our goal in all of our mergers and acquisitions is simply to provide better, more efficient service and a broader coverage area for our customers," Yerger says.

"In the years to come, we'll be looking for more acquisition opportunities that will allow us to expand our products and services even further," Yerger continues. "Since the

company's beginning, we've been on the cutting edge, and we owe it to our customers to stay here. Telecommunications is a business that literally changes overnight, and though the products continue to evolve and develop, ValuePage will always offer the latest available."

THROUGH A SERIES OF ACQUISITIONS AND INTERNAL GROWTH, VALUEPAGE DEVELOPED FROM A SIMPLE PAGING PROVIDER INTO AN INTEGRATED PRODUCT MIX THAT NOW INCLUDES ONE- AND TWO-WAY PAGING, CELLULAR TELEPHONE SERVICE, AND VOICE MAIL (TOP).

"VALUEPAGE IS BUILT AROUND OUR CUSTOMERS' NEEDS AND DESIRE FOR WIRELESS COVERAGE AND SERVICE," SAYS WIRT YERGER III, PRESIDENT OF VALUEPAGE (BOTTOM).

AMONG AN IMPOSING ARRAY OF REGIONAL LAW FIRMS WITH OFFICES IN JACKSON, Baker, Donelson, Bearman & Caldwell is the largest. With more than 220 attorneys and senior public policy advisors and eight offices in two states and the District of Columbia, Baker, Donelson is one of the largest law firms in the Mid-South and the 119th-largest in the country. ✳ The firm that would eventually be known as Baker, Donelson was founded in Memphis, Tennessee, in 1911. In addition to

its Jackson location, Baker, Donelson has offices in Memphis, Nashville, Chattanooga, Knoxville, Tri-Cities Tennessee/Virginia (Johnson City), and Huntsville, Tennessee, and in Washington, D.C.

The firm represents public and private companies on the local, regional, national, and international levels. While its practice is concentrated in the Southeast, its clients' business activities span the nation and the world.

Baker, Donelson–Jackson

The Jackson branch was established in 1995, when Baker, Donelson merged with the health law group of another prominent Jackson law firm. Today, Baker, Donelson's Jackson office includes three practice groups: health law, litigation, and tax and estate planning.

The Jackson office employs 20 attorneys who represent more than 770 clients, including more than 30 hospital- and health-law-related clients. The Jackson office is also home to a strong regional litigation practice—which serves clients in seven

states—and provides tax and estate planning for clients throughout Mississippi.

Practice Areas

Baker, Donelson's overall practice is divided into five major departments and 18 practice areas, including bankruptcy and creditors' rights, commercial lending, communication, corporate, environmental and energy, ERISA and employee benefits, estate planning and probate, health law, intellectual property, international, labor and employment, litigation, mergers and acquisitions, public policy, real estate, securities, tax, and transportation. No other firm in the region can match Baker, Donelson's level of experience across so many practice areas.

The following attorneys are certified as Civil Trial Specialists by the Tennessee Commission on Continuing Legal Education and Specialization: Thomas O. Helton (Chattanooga) and Jill M. Steinberg (Memphis). Randal S. Mashburn (Nashville) is certified as a Business Bankruptcy and

Consumer Bankruptcy Specialist by the Tennessee Commission on Continuing Legal Education and Specialization. Jerry Stauffer is chair of the Litigation Department, which encompasses the areas of employment, environmental, commercial litigation, tort, and bankruptcy and creditors' rights. J. Porter Durham Jr. is chair of the Corporate Department, which encompasses the areas of intellectual property, general corporate/mergers and acquisitions, international, public policy, and securities. Richard G. Cowart is chair of the Health Law Department. Thomas L. Howard is chair of the Tax Department. Robert C. Liddon is chair of the Commercial Lending and Real Estate Department. They are not currently certified in any areas of specialization.

The firm maintains a well-respected public policy and regulatory practice, led by former White House Chief of Staff and Senate Majority Leader Howard Baker. The firm's international practice group, headed by former Secretary of State Lawrence Eagleburger, works with high-level government contacts at home and abroad on behalf of clients with business interests overseas. Ray Mabus, former Mississippi governor and U.S. ambassador to Saudi Arabia, is a member of the international practice group.

A National Leader in Health Law

Largely due to the efforts of its Jackson office, Baker, Donelson has established a successful national practice in health law. Health Law Chairman Richard G. Cowart, one of the original lawyers in the firm's Jackson office, heads the first multidisciplinary team of business and litigation attorneys in the health law industry in the South. These attorneys counsel health care

BAKER, DONELSON, BEARMAN & CALDWELL'S EXPERIENCE WITH SECURITIES INCLUDES A MULTITIERED FINANCING TRANSACTION FOR A MANUFACTURING CONCERN RESULTING IN AN INITIAL PUBLIC OFFERING OF STOCK RANKED AS THE THIRD LARGEST IN THE SOUTHEAST.

systems on mergers and acquisitions, managed care, physician consolidation, and the regulatory aspects of complex health care transactions.

Baker, Donelson has handled more hospital sales than all of the other Mississippi law firms combined, representing the buyer or seller in more than 50 hospital acquisitions in 10 states. By combining the resources of five of the firm's offices, and with the Jackson office taking the lead, Baker, Donelson assisted a client in the simultaneous acquisition, equity private placement, and debt consolidation of the assets of 54 medical practices in 10 states—one of the largest physician combinations in history.

THE STRENGTH OF A REGIONAL FIRM

The size and scope of the firm place an abundance of resources at its clients' disposal. From a simple real estate transaction to complex class action litigation, Baker, Donelson offers the experience and technology needed to handle virtually any legal matter, regardless of size.

A sophisticated communications system and computer network allow instant communication between attorneys in all of the firm's regional offices, as well as immediate access to industry information and research databases. Baker, Donelson's attorneys can tap into a large base of industry and legal experience with the stroke of a key,

which means faster turnaround time and comprehensive, cost-effective service for their clients. In addition, attorneys can link with clients to share and transport documents and to aid in large case management.

Baker, Donelson is the only Jackson-area firm with an office in Washington, D.C. This branch provides Mississippi clients access to attorneys and senior public policy advisers who have tremendous experience in matters involving the federal government and international issues, and who maintain important contacts in Washington.

Finally, the firm's sheer size allows Baker, Donelson to staff virtually any project, even on short notice. Baker, Donelson attorneys working in different offices often collaborate on a single transaction, providing their clients with the services of the top attorneys in their practice areas.

COMMITMENT TO THE COMMUNITY

Service to the communities in which the firm operates is central to the core values of Baker, Donelson. Each associate attorney donates 100 hours per year of service or pro bono work to community and charitable activities.

Baker, Donelson is a supporter of some 25 civic and charitable organizations, including the Mississippi Museum of Art, Mississippi Opera, Jackson Cancer League, University of Mississippi Medical Center Children's Hospital, Mississippi Easter Seal Society, Willowood Developmental Center, University of Mississippi Law School, Mississippi Food Network, Habitat for Humanity, March of Dimes, and United Way.

Exceptional service—to both its clients and its communities—is the hallmark of Baker, Donelson.

PHOTOGRAPHERS

STEVE BAKER is an internationally published photographer who has contributed to more than 100 publications. With a degree in journalism from Indiana University, he is the proprietor of Highlight Photography in Indianapolis, specializing in assignments for such clients as Eastman Kodak, Nike, Budweiser, the U.S. Olympic Committee, and Mobil Oil, which has commissioned seven exhibitions of his work since 1994. Baker is the author/photographer of *Racing Is Everything*, and he contributed to Towery Publishing's *Indianapolis: Crossroads of the American Dream*, *Baltimore: Charm City*, *Chicago: Heart and Soul of America*, and *Nashville: City of Note*.

GEOFFREY ELLIS is a native Californian who moved to Memphis in 1997 after spending 11 years in Miami, Gainesville, and Jacksonville. A graduate of the University of North Florida with a degree in graphic design, he currently works for Towery Publishing as an art director. Ellis specializes in graphic design, freelance photography, and working with Super 8mm film. He also enjoys collecting 8mm and 16mm films, cameras, and LP records. His images appeared in Towery's *Jacksonville: Reflections of Excellence* and *Chicago: Heart and Soul of America*.

ENRIQUE ESPINOSA, a native of Mexico City, moved to Memphis in 1993, where he attended Rhodes College and received a bachelor's degree in art history. An art director at Towery Publishing, he has also done freelance work for *Agenda* magazine and several Rhodes publications, including the school newspaper and alumni magazine.

DEBRA L. FERGUSON is a self-employed photographer at Southern Images in Brandon, specializing in rural lifestyles and agricultural advertising as well as editorial images. Her stock photography is represented by agencies in California and Europe, and her client list includes major farm publications and a variety of advertising agencies. A graduate of Delta State, she is currently working on "Vanishing Delta," a series of photos exploring places and people in the area.

H.K. HOLLOWAY has been a professional photographer since 1984. After graduating from the Brooks Institute of Photography, she concentrated on commercial work until 1989. An interest in capturing people on film led her to open a studio specializing in black-and-white photography. In addition to teaching photography at Millsaps College, Holloway is concentrating on a decade-long project of photographing such Mississippi writers as Eudora Welty, Richard Ford, Beth Henley, Willie Morris, and Ellen Douglas. A 1994 grant enabled her to take portraits of the homeless, which culminated in a show at the Eudora Welty Library. In 1995, a community arts grant supported her as the director of a project that organized artists and writers to teach in the homeless community.

GREG JENSON, originally from Monroe, Louisiana, moved to the Jackson area in 1988. A graduate of Northeast Louisiana University, he studied graphic design, photography, print-making, pottery, and drawing. In addition to freelancing, he works for the *Clarion-Ledger*. Specializing in photojournalism, Jenson enjoys taking pictures of sports. He has received numerous awards from the Mississippi, Indiana, and Michigan press associations.

EYD KAZERY, a self-employed photographer, enjoys taking pictures of Mississippi people and landscapes, and specializes in multiple-image and black-and-white photography. Originally from Jackson, he is a graduate of Belhaven College. His work is featured at the Suite 103 Gallery in Jackson, Southside Gallery in Oxford, and Bosetti-Taylor Gallery in New Orleans.

STEPHEN KIRKPATRICK, a renowned nature and wildlife photographer based in Jackson, has traveled the globe capturing images of exotic plants and animals. His appreciation of nature and wildlife began during childhood and evolved into a full-time career when his father gave him his first camera in 1981. Since then, Kirkpatrick has published more than 1,600 photographs in such magazines as *Audubon*, *Gray's Sporting Journal*, *Natural History Magazine*, *Ducks Unlimited*, *Outdoor Photographer*, *BBC Wildlife*, *National Wildlife*, and *Sports Afield*. The recipient of many awards, Kirkpatrick has published six books, and currently divides his time between speaking engagements throughout the United States and traveling to the Peruvian Amazon, where he's conducting photography tours and working on his next book.

STEVE BAKER / HIGHLIGHT PHOTOGRAPHY

BUD LEE studied at the Columbia University School of Fine Arts and the National Academy of Fine Arts before moving to the Orlando area more than 20 years ago. A self-employed photojournalist, he was named *Life* magazine's News Photographer of the Year in 1967 and received the Military Photographer of the Year award in 1966. He also founded photographers workshops in Florida and Iowa. Lee's work can be seen in *Esquire*, *Life*, *Travel & Leisure*, *Rolling Stone Magazine*, the *Washington Post*, and the *New York Times*, as well as in Towery Publishing's *Orlando: The City Beautiful*, *Jacksonville: Reflections of Excellence*, and *Treasures on Tampa Bay: Tampa, St. Petersburg, Clearwater.*

TOM ROSTER, a Minnesota native, maintains a home in Mississippi, where he lived for more than 10 years. In addition to operating Roster & Company Photography, Inc., he is represented by Black Star Photo Agency. A freelance editorial and corporate photographer, he won the 1994 Photo of the Year Award from the Mississippi Press Association, which has honored him with some 20 other awards since 1982. Roster's clients include the *New York Times Magazine*, *USA Today*, *Inc.*, *London Sunday Times*, *Profil*, *FDA Consumer*, and numerous other publications.

LEE SCHMID, a native of Long Island, attended the Volkswagen Trade School in New Orleans and the School of Modern Photography in New Jersey before settling in Union, Mississippi. His pictures have been included on numerous baseball cards, as well as in the *Clarion-Ledger*, *Astros Magazine*, and *USA Today*. Schmid has also photographed Sam Donaldson, Hillary Clinton, Steffi Graf, Pat Morita, Hank Aaron, Bob Uecker, and many of the current Major League Baseball players. In addition to building his own house, Schmid has restored 24 Model-A Fords, some Volkswagens, and other special interest cars.

J.D. SCHWALM, originally from Kokomo, Indiana, moved to Jackson in 1984. A graduate of Indiana University with a degree in journalism, he also attended classes at Harlaxton College in England. The senior staff photographer at the *Clarion-Ledger*, Schwalm specializes in location portraits, editorial assignment photography, photojournalism, and documentary photography. His images have appeared in *Sports Illustrated*, *People*, *Time*, *Newsweek*, *USA Today*, and the *New York Times*, and his stock file is represented by UNIPHOTO. Schwalm enjoys traveling the back roads of Mississippi, and is currently working on Web page design and content production.

CAROLYN THORNTON is a freelance photographer and writer from Hattiesburg. Her specialties include travel photography, specifically in the South, and images of steam trains. Thornton has many fond memories of spending childhood summers in New Orleans. Her work has appeared in a variety of national publications, such as the *New York Times*, *Modern Bride*, the *London Free Press*, and the *New Orleans Times-Picayune*, as well as in Towery Publishing's *New Orleans: Rollin' on the River.*

GREGORY WILLIAMS, a lifelong resident of Savannah, graduated from the Savannah Technical Institute and has studied under renowned nature photographer John Earl. In his freelance career, Williams specializes in landscape, unique architecture, and abstract photography, and many of his images are used in chamber of commerce guides across the nation. He has won several regional Sierra Club photo contests and, in 1996, mounted an exhibit titled *Savannah and the Georgia Coast*. His images have also appeared in Towery Publishing's *Seattle: Pacific Gem* and *Jacksonville: Reflections of Excellence.*

JIMMY WINSTEAD, a native of Vicksburg, moved to Jackson in 1994. He studied photography in New York City from 1980 to 1994 and worked as an apprentice in several studios with some of the world's best photographers. Currently self-employed, Winstead specializes in architecture, people, and still-life images. His client list includes a number of architectural firms, several of which have won state awards with his photographs.

HUBERT WORLEY JR. is a lifelong Jacksonian who received a bachelor of fine arts degree from the Atlanta School of Art in 1973. He is currently self-employed.

Additional contributors to *Jackson: The Good Life* include Communication Arts Company, the Mississippi Commission for International Cultural Exchange, Inc., and the Mississippi Department of Archives and History.

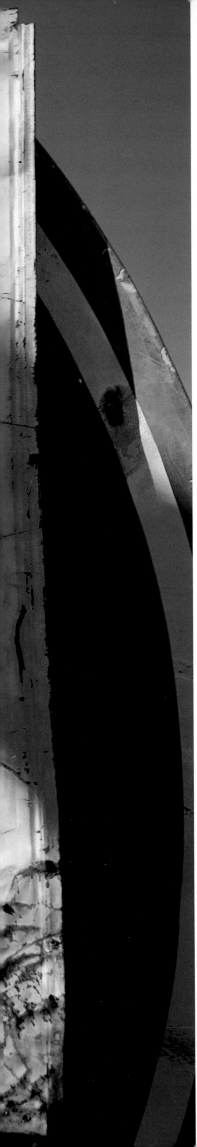

INDEX OF PROFILES

Ya'll
Come Back
Soon